LAW'S EXPRESSION

COMMUNICATION, LAW AND MEDIA IN CANADA

Sheryl N. Hamilton

General Editor: Dr. Logan Atkinson, FCIS

The Carleton University Snapshot Series in Legal Studies.

LexisNexis·

Law's Expression: Communication, Law and Media in Canada
© LexisNexis Canada Inc. 2009
November 2009

Members of the LexisNexis Group worldwide

Canada	LexisNexis Canada Inc, 123 Commerce Valley Dr. E., MARKHAM, Ontario
Australia	Butterworths, a Division of Reed International Books Australia Pty Ltd, CHATSWOOD, New South Wales
Austria	ARD Betriebsdienst and Verlag Orac, VIENNA
Czech Republic	Orac sro, PRAGUE
France	Éditions du Juris-Classeur SA, PARIS
Hong Kong	Butterworths Asia (Hong Kong), HONG KONG
Hungary	Hvg Orac, BUDAPEST
India	Butterworths India, NEW DELHI
Ireland	Butterworths (Ireland) Ltd, DUBLIN
Italy	Giuffré, MILAN
Malaysia	Malayan Law Journal Sdn Bhd, KUALA LUMPUR
New Zealand	Butterworths of New Zealand, WELLINGTON
Poland	Wydawnictwa Prawnicze PWN, WARSAW
Singapore	Butterworths Asia, SINGAPORE
South Africa	Butterworth Publishers (Pty) Ltd, DURBAN
Switzerland	Stämpfli Verlag AG, BERNE
United Kingdom	Butterworths Tolley, a Division of Reed Elsevier (UK), LONDON, WC2A
USA	LexisNexis, DAYTON, Ohio

Library and Archives Canada Cataloguing in Publication

Hamilton, Sheryl N., 1965–
    Expressions law : communication, law and media in Canada / Sheryl N. Hamilton.

Includes bibliographical references and index.
ISBN 978-0-433-45773-2

    1. Freedom of expression--Canada. 2. Freedom of the press--Canada. I. Title.

KE4420.H34 2009   342.7108'53   C2009-906389-1
KF4483.C524H34 2009

Printed and bound in Canada.

General Editor's Introduction

The purpose of the Carleton University Snapshot Series in Legal Studies is to introduce the study of "law in context" to readers unfamiliar with much of the doctrine generally considered prerequisite to such study. This is a challenge of no small significance. Sheryl N. Hamilton's fine book, *Law's Expression: Communication, Law and Media in Canada*, is the second title in the Series, and it accepts the challenge head on. Many of the topics covered in this book are among the most subtle and perplexing issues for practicing lawyers and law students across Canada, yet Dr. Hamilton explains them with a dexterity that readers will surely appreciate. The complexity of the law with respect to hate crimes and obscenity, for example, and the ins and outs of copyright and trademark law, are reviewed in the larger context of the social and philosophical framework out of which legal rules emerge, giving readers just enough of "law as rules" to make sense of this broader context. This is an important accomplishment, one that perfectly realizes the motivation for creation of the Series in the first place.

At Carleton University, we are very pleased to see the development of this Series. Carleton offers some of the most innovative undergraduate and graduate programmes in Legal Studies anywhere, and the Series itself is a product of that innovation. It is our hope that additional titles will be developed and published, such that the Series might start to represent a comprehensive introductory statement of the relationship between social and philosophical context on the one hand, and legal rules on the other. We are very pleased to share this enthusiasm with LexisNexis Canada — its support and patience as the idea of the Series has grown have been central to our plans and key to moving forward.

We are particularly interested in the utility of the texts in the Series as learning tools for students coming to the study of law in context for the first time. But we realize too that the topics covered both in Dr. Hamilton's volume and in the first title in the series, *Private Law, Social Life: An Introduction (2nd Edition)*, are inherently interesting and central to public discourse, meaning that, potentially at least, the Series has appeal to a broader readership, both inside and outside the legal profession. This will be of great significance as the Series evolves, holding out the prospect of a series of accessible texts addressing many of the fundamental legal policy questions at work in Canadian society. *Law's Expression: Communication, Law and Media in Canada* captures that potential perfectly.

Dr. Logan Atkinson, FCIS
General Editor

University Secretary
Carleton University

May 2009

Acknowledgements

My first thank you has to go to my friend and colleague Logan Atkinson who approached me with the idea of doing a textbook in the Law in Context series at Carleton. I was flattered but very clear that I could only take this on if I could do it in a way that reflected my hybrid intellectual identity in legal and communication studies. He encouraged me to do so. I am grateful for your faith in me, Logan, and all your support.

That openness to an interdisciplinary approach continued with the team at LexisNexis Canada. Gian-Luca Di Rocco, Bana Moulhem and Laura Renieri, have all been absolutely fabulous to work with. Thank you for everything. I would work with you again any time!

This text would not have been possible without the amazing research assistance of Sandra Robinson. Thank you so much for the loads of wonderful material, the superior organization system and the ongoing intellectual stimulation and friendship. Emily Truman was available to come in on short notice and provide some much needed additional research at the end of the process. You continue to be a lifesaver. I benefit immensely from the generous financial assistance of the Canada Research Chairs Program and the Office of the Vice-President Research and International at Carleton University. I thank the undergraduate students who inspired this textbook for their energy, their curiosity and their honesty. Colleagues and friends at Carleton University in both the Department of Law and the School of Journalism and Communication make teaching and researching at Carleton an always enjoyable experience.

Finally, to Neil and Brigitte, I couldn't do any of it without you, and wouldn't want to. You are the loves of my life and I dedicate this one to you.

About the Author

Sheryl N. Hamilton is the Canada Research Chair in Communication, Law and Governance at Carleton University. She is an Associate Professor in the Department of Law and the School of Journalism and Communication and teaches in the areas of cultural policy, cultural studies of law, intellectual property, communication theory, cyberculture studies, and gender and technology. She is the author of *Impersonations: Troubling the Person in Law and Culture* (University of Toronto Press, 2009) and a co-author of *Becoming Biosubjects: Bodies. Systems. Technologies*, forthcoming from University of Toronto Press, winter 2009. She has published in journals such as *The Journal of Law, Culture and Humanities*, *Communication Theory*, the *Canadian Review of American Studies*, and *Convergence: The Journal of Research Into New Media Technologies*. Her most recent research project is exploring the constitution of Canada as a "moral nation" through high profile Supreme Court of Canada cases that become cultural events.

Also available in the Series

Private Law, Social Life: An Introduction, 2nd Edition
by Logan Atkinson & Neil Sargent

Table of Contents

Chapter 1

Freedom of Expression in a Media Society

I. INTRODUCTION

Humans are expressive beings — from cave paintings to Baroque music to MySpace — we have things to say. And yet as history has repeatedly shown us, *what* we say, *how* we say it, and *to whom* we say it all have significant social impacts. Think of the symbolic role that Martin Luther's 95 theses nailed to a church door played in relation to the Protestant Reformation, the role that televised news images of the brutalities of the Vietnam War played in mobilizing a generation into protest, or the role that regular email communiqués from Subcommander Marcos played in bringing the plight of indigenous peoples in the Chiapas region of Mexico to the attention of media and governments around the world during the Zapatista revolt.

Upon closer scrutiny of these examples of the power of human expression to shape our world, we can note three very important issues. First, the medium of communication, or the particular technology through which the expression takes place, is important to the geographic reach of the message, to its emotional and intellectual impact upon its audiences, to the speed of its circulation and to the temporality of its life cycle. Second, governments and those in power are very interested not only in the communication of elites, but also in the expressions of ordinary citizens. They understand, respect and sometimes fear the power of democratic communication, with good historical reason. Third and finally, these examples demonstrate that human expression is not something that can be controlled through technology or law; it inevitably leaks out of the boundaries that are placed around it. Human expression and our responses to it are notoriously unpredictable and, as a result, incredibly powerful.

The importance of human communication is recognized by states around the world in the protection of freedom of expression or speech, often in human rights codes and constitutions. These enshrine the long-standing democratic principle that citizens should be able to express ideas and exchange information freely and without interference from the state. The *Canadian Charter of Rights and Freedoms*, for example, protects expression as a "fundamental freedom" in section 2(b):

> 2. Everyone has the following fundamental freedoms ... freedom of thought, belief, opinion and expression, including freedom of the press and other media of communication ...[1].

Prior to the 1982 patriation of the Canadian Constitution and the adoption of the *Charter*, freedom of expression was protected by the courts in Canada through the notion of an "implied bill of rights" and through federal legislation, the *Canadian Bill of Rights* (which lacked constitutional status).[2] Freedom of speech is protected in the First Amendment to the United States Constitution which holds that: "Congress shall make no law ... abridging the freedom of speech, or of the press ...".[3] This difference in language between the American and Canadian Constitutions reflects a difference in how the right is protected, but not whether it is protected.

The Canadian notion of freedom of expression is, at first glance, broader than its American counterpart, including everything from speaking, writing, printing and publishing to physical acts, provided that these express or attempt to express meaning and would not otherwise be illegal (such as violence). The entire process of communication from thought to material representation, to circulation, to receipt is encompassed within the right. However, while we have the right to receive information, we do not have the right to be listened to. The law will not force an audience for our views, but it will protect our right to share them with whoever chooses to listen. Finally, the protection applies not only to political speech but to all forms, including commercial speech such as advertising. While repeatedly protecting commercial speech, courts in Canada have also implied that it is lower on a scale of importance to democratic society than political communication.

Canadian scholars and courts alike have offered a three-part articulation of why we protect freedom of expression. First, there is a basic social value to the production of truth and a robust communicative environment is the best way for a society to negotiate its agreed-upon truths. In other words, the marketplace of ideas is a social good that we should nurture and protect. Second, the right to freely communicate to other citizens is understood as fundamental to producing and preserving democracy and its various institutions. Parliament, legislatures, a free

---

[1]   S.C. 1960, c. 44. Part I of *The Constitution Act*, being Schedule B to the *Canada Act 1982* (U.K.), 1982, c. 11.

[2]   See Moon, Richard. *Constitutional Protection of Freedom of Expression* (Toronto: University of Toronto Press, 2000) for more detail.

[3]   U.S. Const. amend. I.

press and open courts, all require that citizens are free from prior restraint in expressing their diverse views on matters of public interest. This capacity to freely communicate produces, protects and preserves our democratic process. The third rationale is individual, rather than social, and suggests that free expression is integral to human self-fulfillment. In other words, human communication is assumed to be fundamental to how we develop and perform our personal identities in society. It is important to note that the same protections apply to expression which is generally accepted and endorsed by members of society and that which is on the margins of that society's taste culture. The Supreme Court of Canada has confirmed that freedom of expression exists "… to ensure that everyone can manifest their thoughts, opinions, beliefs, indeed all expressions of the heart and mind, however unpopular, distasteful or contrary to the mainstream".[4] And yet, despite this strong protection and significant social value, our freedom to express ourselves is nowhere absolute. Indeed, it is often in situations where our communications are unpopular, distasteful or contrary to the mainstream that debates about the limits of their protection arise.

One of the first ways that our expression is limited, and those limits negotiated, is as a result of the presence of section 1 of the *Charter* itself which provides that: "The *Canadian Charter of Rights and Freedoms* guarantees the rights and freedoms set out in it subject only to such reasonable limits prescribed by law as can be demonstrably justified in a free and democratic society." The federal parliament and the provincial legislatures make the laws that prescribe limits on our expression, for example, by prohibiting child pornography. It is the courts, however, that evaluate if those limits are justified, and this process is called judicial review. They make this determination once they have decided that a law, on its surface, violates a *Charter* right; having done so, they apply what has come to be known as the "Oakes Test". In the case of *R. v. Oakes*,[5] the Supreme Court of Canada outlined the multi-stage test it would use in the application of section 1. The Oakes Test adopts a purposive approach to *Charter* interpretation. This means that the Court will ask, "what does the *Charter* mean in the context of Canadian society as a whole?" This is in contrast with (and includes) relying upon the dictionary meanings of the words (the constructive approach). The first element of the test is to determine whether the legislative provision in question is rationally connected to its objective. The second question the Court asks is whether the legislation causes minimal impairment to the right. Is the limit at issue overbroad in its application or effect? The third and final element in

---

[4] *Irwin Toy Ltd. v. Quebec (A.G.)*, [1989] S.C.J. No. 36, [1989] 1 S.C.R. 927 at 968 (S.C.C.).
[5] [1986] S.C.J. No. 7, [1986] 1 S.C.R. 103 (S.C.C.).

the Oakes Test examines the balance between the effects of the provision limiting the *Charter* right and its objective, which must be of sufficient social importance. In other words, the possible positive and negative effects of the provision are weighed.

This section 1 process is one of the key elements that distinguishes the Canadian and American approaches to free expression. Because there is no similar limit built into its Constitution, United States courts have had to read limits into the right itself, and have been reluctant to do so except in the most extreme instances. In Canada, there are virtually no limits on the right as stated in section 2(b), but the courts have frequently found that legislative limits on free expression meet the section 1 test.

In addition to the possible constitutional limits on all *Charter* rights provided in section 1, there are a number of instances where governments have made laws limiting our freedom of expression. In Canadian society, we have decided that some forms of communication are harmful to others and should be prohibited, that some forms of communication are property and can no longer be used freely by everyone, that some forms of communication should be specifically encouraged over others, or that some means of communication need to be regulated or controlled for the greater good. In short, there are myriad limits on how we can express ourselves and communicate with each other, and almost all of these are enacted and performed through laws governing expression. This book is an exploration of some of those limits. More broadly, it is an examination of how law and expression intersect in a media society. It examines the ways in which our disputes over what is acceptable expression, over who is an acceptable speaker and over what media we can use to speak, all work to define us as a society. Some of these limitations are technical and not particularly controversial, while others have been at the heart of some of our most dramatic moral struggles. But given the significance of communication to individual self-fulfillment and the proper workings of democratic society, the stakes of expression's encounter with the law are high, and they are stakes that affect all of us, every day.

Too often texts exploring media and the law or communication and the law focus exclusively on journalists. While journalists are extremely important to the role that communication plays in democratic society, and have been a focus of government and court scrutiny on many occasions, they are not the only individuals affected by the laws governing media, communication and expression. This is not therefore, a "how-to" manual for media practitioners, although I hope it will be of use to them. It is aimed at students of law, legal studies, and communication and media studies, and is therefore broader in scope. The ways in which the law shapes the practices of journalism and hence our mass mediated environment will be explored in detail in Chapter 2, but we will also take up various sites where their everyday citizens encounter legal limits on expression, whether they always realize it or not. We do not take up issues of interpersonal or private communication because these are domains that the law, for the most part, does not seek to regulate. We will, however, examine the ways in which we are moving into a world where communication is increasingly being treated as a form of private property and our access to it is being limited on that basis. In Chapter 3 we will take up the explosions of activity in the domains of copyright and trademark law. Some of the more spectacular moments of limiting expression have taken place through the criminal law and, more specifically, limitations on obscenity and hate speech. Chapter 4 will explore how deviance and marginality are produced through criminalizing expression — how society clearly says, "we reject this way of speaking or behaving" — but also how more positive forms of community can be supported and defined. In Chapter 5 we will examine still another way in which expression and law intersect when we ask the following questions. How is the law expressed to us? What is the place of media technology in the courtroom? And how is our knowledge of law and the legal system shaped by both the news media and popular culture? Finally, Chapter 6 will offer some concluding thoughts and some conceptual guideposts for making sense of our volatile communicative future.

This is the most exciting time in history to be studying communication, law and media. To illustrate, let's think about a typical day in the life of an average Canadian undergraduate university student, focusing in particular on her mediated communication practices. Shortly after getting up in the morning, she uses a laptop (or cellphone or personal digital assistant (PDA)) to check her email. She has an email account through her university, but also has a free web-based email account. She has a message from a friend providing a link to a YouTube video which she watches on her cellphone over breakfast. After packing up her laptop computer for school, she gets on the bus and like most other passengers, puts on her earphones and turns on her MP3 player. She listens to her favourite music, some of which she purchased through an online site, and some of which she downloaded for free using file-sharing software. In her classroom, laptop computers are being put to a variety of uses: some students are looking at the PowerPoint slides that the professor posted to the online learning system accessible only by members of the class; others are looking up something on Wikipedia for a class paper; some are surfing the web; while others are on Facebook chatting with friends. A student in the back row is sending a link to a racy website to a friend on his cellphone. After downloading a second lecture as a podcast, our student gets back on the bus, this time playing a game on her cellphone as she travels. Finally, she arrives home where she curls up in front of her television to relax, having programmed her personal video recorder (PVR) to record her two favourite programs which were both broadcast the night before in the same time slot.

This is not an atypical example of the imbrication of digital and traditional forms of media into our lives, and we can glean a number of interesting patterns from it. We are consuming and interacting with a greater variety of media for increasing amounts of time each day. Our media content used to be delivered to us on dedicated channels and we consumed that content on specific devices. Now that content can be digitized, it is "platform neutral". It is mobile and we consume it through an increasing array of media technologies. We have not abandoned traditional mass media such as television, radio and newspapers which broadcast the same message to many, as many early commentators worried, but our means of accessing, and our habits around, their consumption have changed dramatically. The temporality of our consumption has changed; we access our media content on *our* schedule, not on that of the media corporation offering the content. And those media corporations are changing. Different producers used to provide different services; however, now a service-provider like Rogers, for example, provides my cable television, Internet and standard and cellular telephony — a phenomenon known as cross-media ownership. The production of mass media content has exploded in order to try to meet the demand, but personal media content has grown even more exponentially. As well, the line between mass and personal media is blurring with blogs, reporters' tweets, wikis, interactive television, and so on. Our social interactions are now often mediated through the same technologies that we are using to consume cultural content. We have become active participants in circulating and producing media content through networks organized around issues of taste, rather than income demographic or geographical region.

Sometimes these changes are described by the term "convergence", although all too often convergence is used to refer only to the ways that media technologies are coming together as a result of networked and digital communication. Convergence is not only a technological phenomenon. Like Henry Jenkins, I suggest that convergence represents a broader cultural shift.[6] Our attitudes towards media consumption and our roles within it have changed. We have come to expect a wider array of choice in media content available to us. Indeed, "choice" has become the primary positive value in the current media environment. We expect our

---

[6]   Jenkins, Henry. *Convergence Culture: Where Old and New Media Collide* (New York: New York University Press, 2006).

media content to be easily accessible and inexpensive (or even free). We think of ourselves as much more active players in the communicative process and, therefore, limitations — whether technological, corporate or governmental — are not appreciated.

Digitization and cultural convergence have made an impact upon the rationales for state and legal interventions into our communication environment and on our forms of expression, undercutting some and bolstering others. Some legal limitations seem more necessary than ever, while others have seemingly been rendered irrelevant. Law-making frequently happens at a slower pace than the development of new technologies and we are at an historical moment where the legal and regulatory environment is struggling to keep up with changes in technologies, business structures and cultural practices. Interestingly, because of the increasing importance of mediated communication in our daily lives, public knowledge of communication law has likely never been higher. As well, the nature of digital communication means that traditional geographical and state boundaries of distribution, circulation and consumption are increasingly porous, if not meaningless. Digital content moves almost instantaneously around the globe, meaning that the effort to regulate our expressive activity, traditionally tied to notions of jurisdiction (defined through geography and sovereignty), must now be a global, not merely national, effort. Jenkins notes: "… we are in an age of media transition, one marked by tactical decisions and unintended consequences, mixed signals and competing interests, and most of all, unclear directions and unpredictable outcomes".[7] We are in an historical moment of incredible flux at the technological, social and legal levels, and that is why it is such an interesting time to be studying the ways in which communication, law and media come together.

It should also be recognized that Canada is a particularly interesting place to be studying communication, media and law. Canada has a relatively open regulatory environment for its communication infrastructure. The Canadian Radio-television and Telecommunication Commission for example, adopted a policy of not regulating new media in Canada. Canadians are well connected in terms of our media given our low population density. For example, data from the last major survey in 2003 indicates that 99 per cent of Canadians have television and 96.3 per cent of houses have a fixed telephone line. Just more than 50 per cent of the population at that point had cellular telephones — a number which has no doubt increased dramatically since that time. Fifty-five per cent of households had Internet access at home with 64 per cent of Canadians

---

[7] *Ibid.*, at 11, drawing upon Ithiel de Sola Pool.

self-identifying as regular Internet users.[8] By 2007, there were six million cable subscribers, 3.3 million digital cable subscribers, and 12.2 million homes were connected to the Internet.[9] However, these same numbers suggest that Canada is not enjoying the same rate of growth as a number of Asian and European nations, and so Canada's global position as one of the best-connected nations appears to be declining. More importantly, in a number of instances, Canada is either a world leader or is pursuing the "path less taken" in its approach to regulating expression relative to the United States, in particular. A good example of this is Canada's very slow path towards copyright reform, in contrast to the hasty adoption in 1998 of the much criticized *Digital Millennium Copyright Act*[10] in the United States. These differences make the Canadian instance an interesting one to Canadians and non-Canadians alike.

A word is necessary on terminology. When scholars refer to "communications law", they typically mean the administration of the laws governing telecommunications and broadcasting in Canada by legislators, regulators and courts. Only sometimes does this include criminalized forms of expression and, very rarely, intellectual property law. If scholars use "media law", they are typically referring to the panoply of laws that shape how the media industries do their work. This includes laws governing access to courts and to documents, contempt, rules around the confidentiality of sources, and so on. This text assumes a very broad definition of communication law, namely one that refers to the multiple ways in which activities of human expression intersect with legal restraints and limits. This is assumed, however, to take place in a mediated environment where the media industries are dominant players in our expressive world and we are increasingly using media technologies to become more engaged in that world. Therefore, this text takes as its focus communication law in media society.

II. LEGAL CONTEXT OF MEDIA REGULATION IN CANADA

In order to understand current communication law issues in media society, it is necessary to be familiar with the historical emergence of the current formal legal-regulatory structure of communications in

---

[8] International Telecommunication Union, *World Telecommunication/ICT Development Report 2006: Measuring ICT for Social and Economic Development* (Geneva: ITU, 2006).

[9] Statistics Canada, *Cable and Satellite Television Industry 2007* (Ottawa: Minister of Industry, 2008).

[10] 112 Stat. 2860 (1998).

Canada. The following four sections mirror the distinctions that the law makes between forms of mediated communication. The first examines the relationship between the law and print given the long history of non-regulation in those domains. Print includes newspapers, as well as magazines and book publishing. The second section reflects the distinction long made in communication law in Canada between carriage and content, or between the medium of transmission and the messages themselves, and takes up carriage, or telephony. The third section explores visual and aural content, specifically through forms of radio and television broadcasting, but also briefly through film. Finally, the fourth section will look at new media, with their hybrid characteristics, and the ways in which the Canadian state has developed its legal-regulatory stance towards them.

Throughout the discussion, we will be able to see that while Canada has seemingly taken a relatively "hands-off" approach to the regulation of media content, and hence expression, upon closer examination, there are a number of ways in which existing structures and regulations, in fact, strongly shape how we can express ourselves. As this chapter will demonstrate, this regulation generally takes the following forms:

1. limitations on the ownership of media industries in Canada;
2. the provision of incentives to produce Canadian content;
3. the regulation of the circulation of Canadian content through technological management; and
4. the direct regulation of content itself.

The first three of these modes are targeted at developing and sustaining viable cultural industries in Canada and focus on the conditions of production and circulation of content. Only the latter specifically targets the quality or nature of the content; however, all of them influence what our communications landscape looks like.

There are three uniquely Canadian "logics" that have dominated the formal legal regulatory framework for communications, namely an overarching and coherent set of values and assumptions that organize regulatory thinking and action. The first is cultural nationalism. There is an ongoing fear that shapes the policy terrain in Canada that our large geographical size, dispersed population, our pluralistic society, our bilingual federal political structure, and so on result in a weakened shared cultural identity. Policymakers worry that many of the traditional ties that bind a nation together through shared values and experience are not present in Canada. The United States has been identified as a central threat with its giant entertainment industries offering a wealth of non-Canadian entertainment content and necessarily undermining our capacity to form a coherent national identity. Policies following this logic try to bolster the production of Canadian content, while holding a particular vision of the nature of that content. The second governing logic is that of technological sovereignty, the belief that we can protect the legitimate and independent political identity of Canada, and control its material and symbolic boundaries through communications technologies spread from coast to coast to coast.[11] The state's control, therefore, is bolstered by its efforts to provide a comprehensive technological infrastructure. Policies adopting this logic prioritize building Canadian-owned communications industries and ensuring their economic survival. A third logic is entering the policy arena as a result of the global ideological shifts beginning in earnest in the 1980s, as well as the pressures from global economic forces and our trading partners. This logic can be called deregulated global competition. Increasingly we see a more hands-off approach towards regulation, combined with the stimulation of competition, and the turn towards open global market forces. Policies following this logic advocate reduced regulatory mechanisms and structures, seeming to take governments out of the communications world and preferring to leave issues to be resolved through competition in the marketplace.

Throughout this chapter, and throughout the whole book, these logics will be evident in the Canadian state's response to expression in a mediated society. Sometimes these different logics operate in a complementary fashion, but increasingly they are understood as being incompatible.

A. Print

In Canada, the government has largely refrained from regulating the print press, or newspapers, as well as the content of books and magazines. Unlike the area of broadcasting, as we shall see later in this chapter, there was no historical argument about the need for the government to administer the limited spectrum or to manage a scarce resource between competitors. My writing a book does not stop anyone else from doing so, and provided that a Canadian individual has the necessary capital, they are able to start up a newspaper. More significantly, however, there is a hard-won relationship between a free press and democratic society with which governments have been reluctant to tamper. An independent free press which can criticize the government of the day is assumed to be a pillar of all current democracies. As the Supreme Court of Canada has said: "[f]reedom of discussion is essential to enlighten public opinion in a democratic state; it cannot be curtailed without affecting the right of the

---

[11]   Here I am borrowing from, and modifying, the notion of "technological nationalism" posed by Charland, Maurice. "Technological Nationalism" (1986), 10(1-2) *Canadian Journal of Political and Social Theory* 196-220.

people to be informed through sources independent of the government concerning matters of public interest."[12]

There is one striking example in Canadian history which is frequently used to emphasize this fundamental relationship. In 1935, the Social Credit government of Alberta, led by pastor-turned-politician William Aberhard, passed *An Act to ensure the Publication of Accurate News and Information*.[13] Aberhard had not been happy with the treatment he and his policies were receiving at the hands of Alberta's newspapers and the bill provided that the government could demand that newspapers publish an official statement by the government in response to any published story about a governmental policy or action. The government could force journalists to identify their sources and to name the author of any published article, editorial or letter. Penalties for thwarting the law included closure of the newspaper. The federal government, which was also no fan of the Social Credit regime, took the atypical step of referring the legislation to the Supreme Court of Canada for a determination as to its constitutionality. A reference is a special application that can be made by the government to the Supreme Court for an opinion on an important and non-political legal matter in the absence of a specific dispute between parties. Often the Court is asked in references to rule upon the constitutionality of proposed or actual legislation.

While the Court found the legislation to be a reprehensible attack on freedom of the press, calling it "retrograde", there was no express provision in the constitution, the *British North America Act, 1867*,[14] to provide a right of freedom of the press or of expression. Instead, the Court found the legislation unconstitutional as it was in fact a form of criminal law, and only the federal government had constitutional jurisdiction over the criminal law. However, the Court wrote at some length about the importance of freedom of expression in a democratic society. Chief Justice Duff held:

> There can be no controversy that [parliamentary] institutions derive their efficacy from the free public discussion of affairs, from criticism and answer and counter-criticism, from attack upon policy and administration and defence and counter-attack; from the freest and fullest analysis and examination from every point of view of political proposals.[15]

Thus, the principle of a free press and freedom of expression for citizens is anchored, not in a rationale of individual rights, but in the broader

12 *Reference Re: Alberta Statutes*, [1938] S.C.J. No. 2, [1938] S.C.R. 100 at 145-46 (S.C.C.).
13 Bill No. 9, 1935 (assented to 23 April 1935). S.A. 1937 (Third Session).
14 30 & 31 Victoria, c. 3 (U.K.).
15 *Reference Re: Alberta Statutes*, [1938] S.C.J. No. 2, [1938] S.C.R. 100 at 133 (S.C.C.).

principles of democratic government. It is interesting to note that in 1938, the *Edmonton Journal* won a Pulitzer Prize for its leadership in the defence of freedom of the press in this case.

Thus, we can see some of the dangers of attempting to regulate newspapers in a democracy. The issue around the regulation of the print press in Canada has not typically been the censorship of content by governments, but rather whether or not the government should intervene in the dramatic concentration of ownership in the Canadian newspaper industry. The concerns are typically expressed about two, often related, phenomena: the concentration of ownership and cross-media ownership. Concentration of ownership occurs when a single entity owns numerous properties within the same type of media, for example, when Southam Corp. owns newspapers in every city in Canada. Cross-media ownership, on the other hand, is when there is ownership of various different types of media by one owner, such as Bell Globe Media owning newspapers, telephones, television, cable and satellites. These types of ownership are seen to be particularly problematic when they take place within the same community or region. Concentration of ownership and cross-media ownership are assumed to reduce the range and quantity of ideas and viewpoints that are circulating in the marketplace of ideas. In 1911, there were 143 daily newspapers, and that number has been radically declining ever since. For example, many argued that Conrad Black's takeovers of a significant number of dailies in Canada during the 1990s resulted in the radical homogenization of content across the country and a swing to political conservatism in the editorial position of all of those papers.

The Canadian government first took on the concentration of ownership issue in 1969 when the Senate, at the urging of Senator Keith Davey, appointed a special committee to examine the mass media, particularly with respect to concentration of ownership. The Davey Committee, which reported in 1970, held that concentration was indeed a significant problem and was likely only going to get worse. The Committee said: "this country should no longer tolerate a situation where the public interest in so vital a field as information [is] dependent upon the greed or goodwill of an extremely privileged group of businessmen".[16] The Committee recommended, among other things, the constitution of a Press Ownership Review Board that could accept or reject mergers and acquisitions of newspapers and periodicals.

The government of the day did not do much with the Davey Committee report upon its release. However, press councils were established in a number of provinces which engage in a form of self-regulation of the

---

[16] Canada, *Report of the Special Senate Committee on Mass Media* by Keith Davey (Ottawa: Queen's Printer, 1971) at 67. Also known as The Davey Report.

newspaper industry and deal with complaints. The Councils are generally recognized to be ineffective with respect to the concentration of ownership issue however, as they have no power to enforce their recommendations. The Canadian government soon had pause to reconsider its policy of non-intervention into newspapers, however, after "Black Wednesday".

On August 27, 1980, the Southam Corporation closed the *Winnipeg Tribune* and the Thomson chain closed the *Ottawa Journal*, leaving Southam in Ottawa and Thomson in Winnipeg with monopolies in those cities. The resulting allegations of collusion resulted in Pierre Trudeau's liberal government bringing conspiracy charges against the two papers under the *Combines Investigation Act*[17] (of which they were later acquitted) and, within one week of the closures, in the striking of the Royal Commission on Newspapers, better known as the Kent Commission after its Chair, Thomas Kent. At the time, Southam and Thomson owned 77 per cent of the daily newspapers in Canada, up from 58 per cent only 10 years before.

The Report, issued in 1981, was generally critical of the newspaper industry, predicting an even greater concentration of ownership in the coming decades. Its proposals were daring: a tax incentive to increase news and editorial content; strong measures to limit concentration of ownership, regional concentration and cross-media ownership; forced divesture of holdings for the two dominant players; and a press rights panel. Not surprisingly, the editorial response in the newspapers across the country was swift and scathing. Kent was attacked personally for his alleged assault on freedom of expression. It became clear almost immediately that it would be politically dangerous to do anything with the recommendations of the Kent Commission. A draft *Daily Newspaper Act* was floated by the government, but was met with stiff opposition in Parliament and was quickly abandoned. In short, the report of the Kent Commission, while identifying and detailing what many believed to be a significant problem, was shelved.

Since that time, there has been at least one other hand-wringing exercise on ownership issues in the newspaper industry that has resulted in virtually no governmental action. In 2006, a Senate report looked at the state of the media and was concerned about concentrated and cross-media ownership. Advocates of a free press often assume the threat to that freedom lies with the state. Historically that may well have been true, but the problem has certainly shifted to the private sector in the modern era. However, these aspects of the print media environment are currently and will remain for the foreseeable future, unregulated. Censorship is a word that no government wants attached to it.

---

[17] R.S., c. C-23.

In the domain of book and periodical publishing, governments in Canada (provincial and federal) have generally focused on incentive structures aimed at building the industry, which have an indirect effect on content. Again, not dissimilarly to the print press, regulation of content directly smacks of censorship. However, attempts to regulate ownership of book and periodical publishing has not met with the same negative response because these domains are not understood as the lifeblood of democracy, but rather as contributing to a robust cultural life in Canada. The support of the publishing industry is governed by the cultural nationalist logic and some critics have suggested that this reproduces certain tendencies of an ideal vision of Canada in the actors and texts which garner more support. Some examples of the type of regulation that exists in the magazine and book publishing sectors are the Book Publishing Industry Development Program through the Department of Canadian Heritage which provides direct assistance to Canadian book publishers. There are parallel importation policies in the area of copyright which protect agreements for the distribution of books in the small Canadian market. There have also been policies made at the international level, too; the *Investment Canada Act*[18] requires foreign investment in the book publishing and distribution sector to be compatible with national cultural policies and of net economic benefit to Canada. As well, like all communications industries in Canada, the legislation supports ownership restrictions.

In 2000, the government launched a Canadian magazine fund to offer support for business development for small magazine publishers, to offer support for arts and literary magazines and to take on industry development projects. This is the latest in a long line of financial incentive policies for Canadian magazines. Legislation such as the *Foreign Publishers Advertising Services Act*[19] requires foreign publishers to sell a certain percentage of their advertising content to Canadian advertisers. Foreign owners are prohibited from purchasing Canadian magazines, there is a postal subsidy provided to Canadian periodicals, and there are tax deductions granted to advertisers in magazines directed to the Canadian market. These initiatives all compensate Canadian media producers for what are perceived to be the deficiencies in the market for Canadian print culture — deficiencies of size, geographic dispersion, competition from other forms of media and significant competition from the American market. And in general, they have been acknowledged as having had a favourable impact upon the sustenance of the Canadian publishing industry.

---

[18] R.S.C. 1985, c. 28 (1st Supp.).
[19] S.C. 1999, c. 23.

B. Telecommunications

Unlike print, telephones, radio, television, cable, satellite and other media have not been exempt from regulation by the Canadian state. The regulatory regime established for these media relied upon, and still reflects, a distinction between what is known as "carriage" and "content". Carriage is the means of communication — the technological systems used to carry and transmit information, whether that is done by means of wire, fibreoptic cable or airwaves. The carriage industry includes telecommunications and cable operators, for example. Content, on the other hand, is the information, text, sound, images, data, video, and so on that are transmitted over the carriage system. This turns the regulatory gaze to broadcasters as producers and suppliers of communicative content. This distinction is reproduced in the two most significant pieces of communication legislation, the *Telecommunications Act*[20] (carriage) and the *Broadcasting Act*[21] (content). Governmental jurisdiction for carriage and content has also been divided between the Ministries of Industry and Canadian Heritage, respectively. While not unique to Canada, the content-carriage distinction results in certain tensions and does not map as easily onto new media as it does to the more traditional forms.

The *Telecommunications Act* tends to address economic and social issues, framing its work as content neutral. The *Broadcasting Act*, on the other hand, contains predominantly cultural goals. This separation implies that the domain of telecommunications has no cultural implications or that it is not cultural, in and of itself. Correspondingly, the *Broadcasting Act*'s focus on content for cultural purposes denies the very real economic and social impacts of the broadcast industries. As well, the distinction assumes that these functions remain in separate industries (telecommunication and cable on the one hand, and television and radio on the other), and increasingly we see companies engaged in activities that cut across the content-carriage distinction. This is the very meaning of cross-media ownership, which, as noted earlier, increasingly dominates the Canadian mediascape.

The *Telecommunications Act* is the most significant formal law governing carriage and it is administered by Industry Canada. It regulates the activities of what it calls "common carriers", companies like Bell Canada, Rogers and Shaw, for example, when they are providing telephone, cable and Internet services. A telecommunication common carrier is defined in the legislation as "a person who owns or operates a

---

[20] S.C. 1993, c. 38.
[21] S.C. 1991, c. 11.

transmission facility used by that person or another person to provide telecommunications services to the public for compensation."[22] It specifically excludes broadcasters and broadcasting activity from its purview. The legislation takes as its guiding principle that high quality communication services should be widely and readily available in both rural and urban areas of Canada and that they should be reasonably priced for all.

Historically in Canada, telecommunications was governed by the *Railway Act*[23] and regulated by the Board of Transport Commissioners (or its predecessor). Carriers were given monopolies over geographic areas in exchange for the commitment to provide minimum service levels, wide access and controlled prices. Similarly, to book and magazine publishing, and as we shall see, to broadcasting, there were limitations on foreign ownership. The carriers were understood to be "natural monopolies" because of the significant initial investments in infrastructure required to set up the telephone system, but which system then resulted in significant reductions in costs as customer numbers increased. A natural monopoly exists when a single business is assumed to be able to provide superior services at lower costs than an open market of competing suppliers would be able or willing to do. The worry was that if left to market forces alone, Canadians in densely populated urban areas would have a wide range of inexpensive telephone services and those in more remote areas would have poorer services at exorbitant prices. Regulation was seen as the solution to this risk. It was this rationale of the natural monopoly, for example, that allowed BCE Inc. (Bell Canada) to become the dominant telephone provider until the 1980s when the appeal of the notion of natural monopolies began to fade in a climate of increasing business and technological convergence and a general global move to deregulation.

Jurisdiction over telecommunications was, until 1989, shared between the federal and provincial governments. Over the 1980s and early 1990s, there was a constitutional tussle between the two levels of governments about whether, with all the technological changes at the time, telephones should be contained within federal government control over telegraphs or "interprovincial undertakings" (projects which cross the borders of one province) or whether they could be considered "local works and undertakings" only, and thus within provincial jurisdiction. In 1989, the Supreme Court of Canada finally awarded exclusive jurisdiction over

---

[22] S.C. 1993, c. 38, s. 2.
[23] 51 Vic. c. 29.

telecommunications to the federal government.[24] A new *Telecommunications Act* was passed in 1993 to reflect this change.

While the hallmark of the regulation of telecommunication in Canada has always been its content-neutrality — it focuses on the principles governing the means of transmission, not the content — telecommunications has been understood as a public good and also as a nation-building technology. While the legislation does not reflect the policy logic of cultural nationalism to nearly the same extent as the regulatory regimes governing broadcasting, it does reproduce the logic of technological sovereignty. The Act's objectives provide:

> 7. It is hereby affirmed that telecommunications performs an essential role in the maintenance of Canada's identity and sovereignty and that the Canadian telecommunications policy has as its objectives:
>
> (a) to facilitate the orderly development throughout Canada of a telecommunications system that serves to safeguard, enrich and strengthen the social and economic fabric of Canada and its regions;
> (b) to render reliable and affordable telecommunications services of high quality accessible to Canadians in both urban and rural areas in all regions of Canada;
> (c) to enhance the efficiency and competitiveness, at the national and international levels, of Canadian telecommunications;
> (d) to promote the ownership and control of Canadian carriers by Canadians;
> (e) to promote the use of Canadian transmission facilities for telecommunications within Canada and between Canada and points outside Canada;
> (f) to foster increased reliance on market forces for the provision of telecommunications services and to ensure that regulation, where required, is efficient and effective;
> (g) to stimulate research and development in Canada in the field of telecommunications and to encourage innovation in the provision of telecommunications services;
> (h) to respond to the economic and social requirements of users of telecommunications services; and
> (i) to contribute to the protection of the privacy of persons.[25]

As can be seen, the logics of both deregulated global competitiveness and technological sovereignty are at play. Unfortunately for policymakers and perhaps for common carriers, these logics are not always compatible. In fact, most of the tensions within the domain of telecommunications result from these sometimes competing, and even conflicting cultural logics. For example, the *Telecommunications Act* provides for Canadian ownership of common carriers: 80 per cent of

---

24 *Alberta Government Telephone v. CRTC*, [1989] 2 S.C.R. 225 (S.C.C.).
25 S.C. 1993, c. 38, s. 7.

the shares of all common carriers must be owned by Canadians (either individuals or corporations). There have been regular proposals to eliminate, or at a minimum, to relax the ownership restrictions on common carriers and open Canada up to a global market in telecommunications service provision, but so far they have not been successful, in part because of concerns generated from the logic of Canadian technological sovereignty. Service providers from outside Canada will not have as one of their objectives linking Canadians to other Canadians in support of a shared national identity and governmental control.

The regulatory agency that manages Canadian common carriers is the Canadian Radio-television and Telecommunication Commission, or the CRTC. It is established and governed by its own legislation, the *Canadian Radio-television and Telecommunications Commission Act.*[26] The CRTC is given a lot of autonomy in how it regulates the telecommunication industries, although its decisions are subject to review by the Commission itself, the federal cabinet and the federal courts. In general, the CRTC's approach to telecommunications regulation has moved slowly and seemingly inexorably towards a greater reliance on market forces and a reticence to overly regulate. Handa *et al.* (2008) suggest that the CRTC has gone through three stages.[27] First, from its inception in 1968 until 1993, it operated as a monopoly regulator, regulating prices and encouraging the building of infrastructure. In its second phase, it became a policy maker, particularly after the 1993 legislation made provision for it to adopt that role. Finally, since the late 1990s, they suggest that it has moved into the role of "expert referee and mediator" where its primary focus has been to ensure competition is sustainable and that consumers' interests are protected.

This shift in logic towards deregulated global competitiveness has led to more collaboration with industry to achieve certain economic goals. Sometimes this increasingly close relationship with industry has resulted in accusations that there has been "market capture" of the CRTC, namely that it has ceased to be an objective and independent regulatory body and has been co-opted by industry or political agendas. The CRTC would counter that it believes that the only way to ensure a competitive and dynamic Internet service and digital communications economy in Canada is to embrace a competitive telecommunications approach.

Certainly in recent years, we have witnessed a decline in, although not the death of, the technological sovereignty way of thinking. There have been regular calls from industry and commentators alike to revise the

---

[26] R.S.C. 1985, c. C-22.

[27] Handa, Sunny, Richard Janda, David Johnstone & Charles Morgan. *Communications Law in Canada* (Markham, ON: LexisNexis Canada, 2008).

telecommunications regulatory structure in Canada to reflect this shift, but as recently as April 2005, the federal government stated publicly that it was not necessary to revise the *Telecommunications Act*, the *Broadcasting Act* or the *Canadian Radio-television and Telecommunications Commission Act*. But the urging continues. In 2006, for example, the Telecommunications Policy Review Panel, after a detailed analysis, recommended significant changes to the current telecommunications environment, including less regulation, more competition, and the relaxing of the foreign ownership provisions. In 2009, the CRTC has once again undertaken a review of its telecommunication regulations that is ongoing at the time of this writing. It will be interesting to see if the delicate balancing of the goals of technological sovereignty and deregulated global competitiveness can be maintained in the future.

C. Visual and Aural Content

While the laws governing carriage of media services in Canada shape access to technologies which enable freedom of expression, the continued regulation of media content throughout Canadian history much more directly engages our rights to express ourselves. Here the cultural nationalism logic has been dominant, suggesting the support and regulation of media content by government has been necessary to produce, maintain, bolster, circulate and protect Canadian culture and identity against the seeming threat of the American media behemoth. The *Broadcasting Act* is a significant statement of that principle and regulates the activities of all entities which provide content to the public by means of the airwaves, namely radio, television, cable, digital T.V. and satellite-based broadcast services. The story of how we got to our current regulatory situation is a little bit more fraught than it is in the domain of telecommunications and reflects the political currents of the day much more directly. It involves a fairly regular back and forth between government studies and broadcasting legislation.

Radio broadcasting became a concern of the Canadian government in the first decade of the 20th century. It passed several pieces of legislation in those early decades to license radiotelegraph stations, in part because stronger American stations were being picked up in Canada by Canadians who owned receivers and were eager for content. Commercial radio formally began in Montreal in 1920, but developed slowly. The Canadian National Railway was the first public radio broadcaster, established in 1923 to provide radio to its passengers. The 1920s were a volatile time however, for fledgling Canadian media industries. Canada was being flooded with media content of all sorts from the United States: magazines, books, newspapers and radio broadcasts. While this concerned the government of the day, all available historical evidence confirms that consumers were quite happy to receive and consume the American broadcasts and other media content.

The government was concerned enough about the threat to Canada's cultural identity to appoint the Royal Commission on Radio Broadcasting, better known as the Aird Commission, after its Chair, John Aird. Its mandate was to "examine into the broadcasting situation in the Dominion of Canada and to make recommendations to the Government as to the future administration, management, control and financing thereof". The Aird Commission famously recommended — in a report that was an atypically succinct nine pages — that broadcasting in Canada, not unlike telecommunications, be considered a public service, but with all stations owned and operated by a national company. The adoption of this report by the Canadian government set the terms of a number of regulatory battles to come — including those between the federal and provincial governments and between the private and public broadcasters — which shape the broadcasting terrain to this day.

First, the provision of any national public radio corporation would be problematic given that, unlike the technological aspects of radio, which were within federal jurisdiction to govern, the regulation of the content of media would fall to the provinces. In order to resolve the inevitable disputes which were looming on the horizon, the federal government submitted a reference to the Supreme Court of Canada in 1931. In *Re Regulation and Control of Radio Communication in Canada*, the Supreme Court of Canada held by a margin of 3 to 2 that broadcasting was within federal jurisdiction.[28] At this time, however, the Supreme Court of Canada was not the last court of appeal for Canada, but rather the Judicial Committee of the Privy Council in England had the final say (and did so until 1949). It agreed with the Supreme Court and shortly afterwards in 1932, the federal government proposed Canada's first significant broadcasting legislation: the *Canadian Radio Broadcasting Act*.[29] The legislation closely followed the recommendations of the Aird Commission. It created a federal broadcasting system and a regulatory agency, the Canadian Radio Broadcasting Commission (CRBC), that would operate as both a broadcaster and an independent regulator of the broadcasting field. The hope of the government was that a system could be successfully developed in Canada modelled on the British Broadcasting Corporation (BBC) in the United Kingdom.

---

[28] [1931] S.C.J. No. 33, [1931] S.C.R. 541 (S.C.C.), affd [1932] J.C.J. No. 1, [1932] 2 D.L.R. 81 (P.C.).

[29] S.C. 1932, c. 51.

Not at all surprisingly, the CRBC was a complete failure. There were three primary reasons for this. First, it was underfunded given that Canada was suffering from the Great Depression; second, it was playing an untenable dual role as both regulator and the object of regulation; and third, private broadcasting was not so easily going to be stopped. These challenges led to the 1936 broadcasting legislation. In the place of the CRBC, the new Act created the Canadian Broadcasting Corporation (CBC). Private and public broadcasting stations were permitted, but CBC content was delivered over private stations. Once again, however, the CBC was still playing a dual regulatory role and it was better funded than the private stations, with more powerful stations. In other words, it was set up from the beginning to be dominant. As well, the CBC's strength was enhanced by its role as a national broadcaster in a time of increased nationalism during World War II; it built up a strong and loyal audience base.

However, the tensions with the private sector continued after the War. The Canadian Association of Broadcasters (CAB) had formed to give voice to the private broadcasters and it had two main messages that it communicated repeatedly to the Canadian government. CAB protested the CBC's ongoing conflict of interest as regulator and broadcaster and it wanted the role of private broadcasters in the overall Canadian broadcasting system clarified. In response to concerns, not only within broadcasting, but with cultural sovereignty more broadly, in 1949 the Canadian government appointed the Royal Commission on National Development in the Arts, Letters and Sciences — what would come to be known as the Massey Commission. Not unlike Aird before it, the Massey Commission had a strong cultural nationalist perspective and recommended one integrated broadcasting system.

The problems of broadcasting in Canada were about to get more complicated, however. The United States had started to develop television in the late 1940s and regular broadcasting began in Canada in 1952. Television, it turned out, was wildly popular with Canadians. Canada had the fastest growth in television set purchase in the world with 2.3 million households owning a television by 1956.[30] Again, it appeared that Canadian cultural identity was under assault and so in 1955 the federal government established the Royal Commission on Broadcasting, better known as the Fowler Commission. Its mandate was to consider the problem of financing the Canadian broadcasting system and the respective roles of private and public broadcasters. In its 1957 Report, Fowler recommended a publicly supported Canadian broadcasting system, asserting that it was essential to protect Canadian cultural identity from

---

[30] Handa *et al.*, *supra*, at 6.11.

American influence. It also recommended the creation of a new regulatory agency, separate from the CBC, which would work as a partner with the CBC.

Motivated by the Commission Report, the government enacted the *Broadcasting Act, 1958*[31] which called for the integration of private and public broadcasters to form a national broadcasting system and finally set up a regulatory agency separate from the CBC, namely the Board of Broadcast Governors (BBG). This legislation was the first to articulate detailed policy objectives for the CBC and for the BBG, most of which embraced the cultural nationalism logic. The BBG finally opened up the field to private broadcasters to compete with the CBC. But before long problems arose again. While the CBC was no longer in a direct conflict of interest, it did have a differential and privileged status. The BBG was regulating private stations and the CBC was regulating itself, eschewing the BBG's authority. As well, the BBG was structurally weak. It was charged with ensuring that broadcasters met the policy objectives contained in the Act, but there was no statutory basis for it to enforce this.

After yet another examination of and report on broadcasting — this time, Fowler's Committee on Broadcasting — new legislation was again passed in 1968. The *Broadcasting Act, 1968*[32] proposed a complete national broadcasting policy, created the Canadian Radio-television Commission (CRTC) and recognized the role of private broadcasters, thereby setting up the parameters of the current regulatory framework. Broadcasting and telecommunications regulation were brought under the authority of one agency, renamed the Canadian Radio-television and Telecommunication Commission in 1976. This turned out to be a timely move as the issue that dominated broadcasting regulation for the next decade was the impact of satellites. Satellite technology seemed to pose a huge threat to national cultural sovereignty — signals could be sent and received from all over the world and they did not respect national regulatory borders. Thus, there were content issues. At the same time, satellite-based broadcasting seemed to open up a world of choice to consumers, offering an ideal means to link the country together; however, it was constrained by being a limited resource — carriage issues. The consideration of these issues was taking place in the context of the international deregulation of all markets. Thus we can see all three of the regulatory logics in play at this time, but not necessarily in equal measure. It is in this period as well, that the long slow decline of the CBC began as a result of consistent budget cuts; private broadcasters were now dominating the

---

[31] S.C. 1958, c. 22.
[32] S.C. 1968, c. 25.

market and their connection with the logic of cultural nationalism had always been much more tenuous.

As this was yet another period of flux, the conservative government appointed a task force to conduct a full-scale review of broadcasting policy. The Caplan-Sauvageau Report, surprisingly to many, recommended the continuation of the basic policy framework. It maintained a cultural nationalism discourse and endorsed a public broadcasting model despite the surrounding context of market-driven policy-making and the rise in ascendance of the logic of deregulated global competitiveness. It was a contrast with the previous Applebaum-Hébert Committee Report (1982) which had recommended substituting the market for an administered regime in broadcasting.

The 1991 *Broadcasting Act*[33] reflects these tensions. It contains 20 un-wieldy policy objectives that run the gamut from Canadian ownership of the broadcasting system to bilingualism, to "safeguard[ing], enrich[ing], and strengthen[ing] the cultural, political, social and economic fabric of Canada". It supports the production of Canadian-authored content and seeks content that offers information, education, entertainment and "enlightenment" to all Canadians, recognizing their diversity. And thus, in the late 1990s, yet another inquiry examined broadcasting policy, this time led by the CRTC. It reiterated the need to support Canadian content, but also began the transition into new media policy, as we shall see in the subsequent section. However, certainly the experience with regulation in Canadian broadcasting reveals the tenacity of the cultural nationalism logic.

In addition to the legislation, to understand how broadcasting is regu-lated in terms of its impact upon freedom of expression, one must turn to the work of the CRTC. The CRTC issues licences to broadcasters (which, similarly to common carriers, must be Canadian owned), and no one can operate a broadcast undertaking without a licence. Even though the CRTC has the power to cancel, suspend or refuse to renew a broadcast-ing licence for breach of content-based commitments made as a condition of licence (for example, not enough Canadian content or content which is offensive), rarely has it done so. There is one striking example of an exception, however. CHOI-FM Quebec was a radio station that prided itself on its controversial content, featuring a number of "shock jocks". Commenting, for example, on the mistreatment of a patient in a psychiat-ric hospital, one of the hosts said, "Why don't they just pull the plug on him? He doesn't deserve to live. The guy's a freaking burden on society." He later suggested that the patients should be euthanized. "Fill up the rooms, and then there'd be a switch, and once every four months, they

---

[33] S.C. 1991, c. 11.

press the button and just a little bit of gas comes out, and then you go in and pick it all up and put it in bags." When commenting on a female television network host in Quebec, one of the jocks said, "the size of the brain is not directly proportional to the size of the bra", later referring to the same journalist as a "cat in heat". Another complaint noted that international students from Africa attending Laval University had been referred to as the children of "cannibals". Not surprisingly, many complaints had been laid against the station with the Canadian Broadcast Standards Council.

As a result of the station's refusal to change its practices in response to the many complaints, in 2002 the CRTC took the dramatic step of issuing a two-year licence to CHOI rather than the standard seven-year renewal. CHOI continued its style of programming and in 2004, for the first time, the CRTC denied a licence renewal on the basis that the broadcaster did not meet the "high standards" of broadcasting. This set off a maelstrom of criticism that the CRTC was violating freedom of expression and censoring a broadcaster, regardless of how distasteful most people found the content. Genex Communications, the owner of the station, claimed that it was being censored and that its right to freedom of expression was being violated, but the Federal Court upheld the CRTC decision in 2005. Ultimately because the company made arrangements with another station to work together under its licence, the Supreme Court of Canada never heard the appeal for which Genex filed notice.

The CRTC could make the decision that it did in the Genex case because of the provisions in the *Radio Regulations*[34] that place limits on the content of broadcasting. There are similar provisions in the *Television Broadcasting Regulations*.[35] They are broader and less detailed than the criminal law limits that we will discuss in Chapter 4. Media outlets cannot broadcast "obscene or profane" words or images.[36] As well, the regulations address what has become known as hate speech. Broadcasters are prohibited from airing "abusive comment" or "abusive pictorial representation" that is likely to expose a group or individual "to hatred or contempt on the basis of race, national or ethnic origin, colour, religion, sex, sexual orientation, age or mental or physical disability".[37] The constitutionality of these regulations had been challenged and upheld as a reasonable limit on freedom of expression.[38] However, for the most

---

[34] 1986, SOR/86-982.

[35] 1987, SOR/87-49.

[36] *Radio Regulations, 1986*, SOR/86-982, s. 3(c) and *Television Broadcasting Regulations, 1987*, SOR/87-49, s. 5(1)(c).

[37] *Radio Regulations, 1986*, SOR/86-982, s. 3(b) and *Television Broadcasting Regulations, 1987*, SOR/87-49, s. 5(1)(b).

[38] *CJMF-FM Ltee v. Canada (CRTC)*, [1984] F.C.J. No. 244 (F.C.A.).

part, not wanting to play the censor, the CRTC has stayed well clear of enforcing content quality issues for Canadian broadcasters.

From the mid-1980s until the early 1990s, the CRTC transferred the responsibility for monitoring the quality of broadcast content to a regime of industry self-regulation, including organizations such as the Canadian Broadcast Standards Council (CBSC) and Advertising Standards Canada (ASC). The CBSC was established in 1991 and monitors industry adherence to a series of voluntary codes developed by the CAB governing ethics, gender portrayal and violence. The ASC, too, encourages its members to adhere to a general ethical code, a gender code, a guideline on advertising to children and limitations pertaining to the advertising of alcoholic beverages. These guidelines are not completely toothless, although they are complaint-initiated, meaning that scrutiny is only applied once there are concerns expressed by the public. In the mid-1990s enough complaints were received about the violent nature of a live-action television series aimed at children, *Mighty Morphin' Power Rangers*, that it was taken off the air. *The Howard Stern Show* was voluntarily pulled from some Canadian radio stations after a significant number of complaints from the public about its sexist, racist and inappropriate content. The television station *Al Jazeera Arabic* has also been investigated, but no action against it was ultimately taken.

While the CRTC gave the evaluation of the quality of content to industry self-regulation, it still regulates broadcasting content in other ways, although most of these have not been particularly controversial. For example, it has made provision to require cable providers to substitute a local or regional Canadian cable television station if the program is aired at the same time on a more distant station. This permits the inclusion of region-relevant advertising and the resulting economic support of local stations. Clearly a choice is being made that local content is better than distant, and particularly, American content. Another strategy for strengthening Canadian cultural production has been to stipulate Canadian content quotas, popularly known as the "CanCon rules". These were first established in 1959 and then strengthened in 1972. For example, regular stations must devote 60 per cent of their broadcasting year and 50 per cent of their evening broadcasting to Canadian programs. On commercial radio, 35 per cent of popular music must be Canadian during day and night time slots. Specific rules have also been developed to stimulate particular genres of Canadian programming that are typically less popular: drama, music, long-form documentary, regional programming, and so on. These rules are combined with a financial structure that essentially taxes stations to make contributions to production funds. The CBC is under stricter requirements for Canadian content, and meeting those requirements has become increasingly difficult in recent decades with the dramatic cuts in budget the CBC has faced.

Thus, it is safe to say that with respect to broadcasting content, the CRTC plays a relatively "muted role" to borrow Robert Martin's phrase,[39] preferring positive incentive structures to shape future content, rather than prior restraints and punitive measures on existing content. It is then the media industry, itself, which controls content, but it does so in a legal context that provides several restraints, as will be discussed in subsequent chapters. It will be interesting to see, however, whether the rationale of cultural nationalism continues to dominate after the 2009 review of broadcasting policy that is currently under way at the CRTC, similar to the telecommunications consultations, at the time of this writing.

There are two other ways in which visual media content is regulated in Canada: through the various policies shaping film and television production, and through provincial film classification boards, both of which have been strongly guided by the cultural nationalist logic. The approach of the federal government towards film has been twofold: one public and one private. The first strategy has been the direct financial support for the production of film content through the creation of and ongoing funding provided to the National Film Board (NFB). The NFB was created in 1939 with a mandate that communications scholar Zoë Druick describes as "famously vague", namely "to help Canadians in all parts of Canada to understand the ways of living and problems of Canadians in other parts".[40] Its role has changed over the decades from a war propaganda office during World War II, to an educational film provider in the 1950s, to supporting women filmmakers in the 1960s and 1970s, to supporting minority and First Nations filmmakers in the 1980s and 1990s.[41] Not surprisingly, as a government-funded source of media content, similar to the CBC, the NFB is regularly accused of various forms of bias, and has fought with the government in several instances over attempts to censor its films. In the 1970s, several films portraying Quebec nationalism were edited or cut by the NFB as too separatist in orientation. In 1982 and again in 1992, the NFB fell afoul of veterans groups in its representations of World War II and was even taken to court on defamation charges (which ultimately failed). In both instances, the government, through the Senate, intervened in the dispute and required the films be changed and/or removed from the broadcast cycle.

---

[39] Martin, Robert. *Media Law*, 2d ed. (Toronto: Irwin Law, 2003) at 17.

[40] Druick, Zoe. *Protecting Canada: Government policy and documentary film at the National Film Board of Canada* (Montreal and Kingston: McGill Queen's University Press, 2007).

[41] *Ibid.*

The second regulatory approach to film in Canada, similarly to the print media, has been to provide financial incentives of varying sorts to private film and television makers to develop and support an indigenous industry. Often producers combine resources obtained from federal production funds with those received from parallel provincial programs. Examples include the Canadian Television and Film Development Fund which was first established in 1967 and renamed Telefilm Canada in 1984. Along with financial support for the private film production sector, Telefilm Canada also administers the Canadian Television Fund which is designed to support the creation and broadcast of Canadian television programming.

Again, as with the various initiatives instituted in the Canadian books and periodicals industry, the incentives for film have generally been credited with strengthening the Canadian film and television production industry. Typically, they do not really implicate issues of freedom of expression. A recent exception, however, was Bill C-10 proposed by the Conservative government in October of 2007 to make amendments to the *Income Tax Act*,[42] specifically the provisions with respect to tax credits for Canadian-made productions. The proposed amendment would have given the power to the Heritage Minister to withdraw tax credits from a Canadian-made production if the film was deemed to be "contrary to public policy". That section of the bill was denounced by members of the film and television industry, who labelled it censorship and a violation of freedom of expression. The provision eventually died on the order paper, perhaps in part due to the significant opposition to it, but it did serve as a reminder that even policies aimed at bolstering an industry can quickly become limits on freedom of expression through the targeted criteria used to provide that funding.

More controversially, and more directly affecting the freedom of expression of everyday Canadians has been the work of provincial film classification boards. The Supreme Court of Canada held in 1976 that the power to censor films lies with the provinces. Every province except Newfoundland and Labrador has a film classification board (or uses one of a neighbouring province) that rates films and videos shown within that jurisdiction. Typically films are assessed in relation to violent and sexual content. Film ratings are awarded, permitting consumers to make in-formed choices. Warnings are placed on some films due to their extreme content and sometimes a jurisdiction will refuse to permit a film to be screened at all or require its editing. These agencies have been criticized over the past century for their subjective, sometimes seemingly random and often socially conservative approach to controlling access to filmic

---

[42] R.S.C. 1985, c. 1 (5th Supp.).

expression. Although it is likely fair to say that most provincial boards have been moving away from direct censorship, there are still some exceptions that mobilize public awareness around freedom of expression.

A recent example was Catherine Breillat's film, *Fat Girl* (2001) which is a coming of age story about two teenage sisters. It had been distributed in Europe, Britain and the United States without issue. It screened at the 2001 Toronto International Film Festival and was approved for distribution by the film review boards of Quebec, Manitoba, Alberta and British Columbia. The Ontario board demanded cuts in scenes portraying adolescent nudity and a rape. The review board's position was upheld on two appeals. The film's distributors refused to make the cuts and were going to take the Ontario board to court, challenging the constitutionality of the *Theatres Act* in relation to the right of freedom of expression. The review board promptly had a change of heart, reconsidered the film and it was approved for distribution in Ontario without the cuts. While such incidents are increasingly rare, they do occur and affect both the film creators' rights to freedom of expression and that of audience members.

D. New Media

New media are the fourth component of the regulatory regime governing communication in Canada. In many ways a hybrid of content and carriage, new media challenge many of the traditional frameworks and boundaries in which more traditional media have been understood and administered. Because it involves the digitization of all forms of mediated content, interactivity between producer, distributor and consumer, and interconnected networks crossing provincial and national borders (thus blurring jurisdictional boundaries), in many ways, new media are a regulator's nightmare; and jurisdiction for that nightmare in Canada has been assumed to lie with the CRTC, although this issue has never been litigated or legislated.

The CRTC defines new media as "encompassing, singly or in combination, and whether interactive or not, services and products that make use of video, audio, graphics and alphanumeric text; and involving, along with other, more traditional means of distribution, digital delivery over networks interconnected on a local or global scale".[43] New media have been the subject of extensive study and scrutiny on the part of the CRTC since the early 1990s when it was first charged with examining what was then called the "Information Highway". The first wave of analysis culminated in the 1995 report entitled, *Competition and Culture on*

---

[43]   CRTC, Public Notice 1999-84 (Ottawa: 17 May 1999) at para. 14.

Canada's Information Highway: Managing the Realities of Transition (better known as the "Convergence Report").[44] That process recognized that the Internet had shifted from being primarily a research network to an interactive space dominated by commercial activity. The Report reflected the simultaneous presence of all three Canadian communication regulatory logics: cultural nationalism, technological sovereignty and deregulated global competitiveness. These tensions were also revealed in the simultaneously cultural and economic objectives in the CRTC Vision Statement of 1997. This document outlined the CRTC's vision for the information age and contained four "Vision Thrusts":

1. promoting an environment in which existing and new communications services are available to Canadians;
2. ensuring a strong Canadian presence in content that fosters creative talent and reflects Canadian society, including its linguistic duality and cultural diversity;
3. promoting choice and diversity of high-quality communication services; and
4. fostering strong competitive and socially responsive communication industries.

To this end, it advocated a shift towards a more economistic model of communications in Canada, including more collaboration with industry players and more competition. The CRTC clearly stated that it was shifting its model of regulation: in relation to content, from one of protection to promotion; in relation to choice, from constraint to competition; in relation to regulatory approach, from detailed regulation to broad parameters; and in relation to its process, from a judicial to a collaborative process.

The CRTC held a series of hearings in 1998-99, dubbed the "New Media Hearings" and many were expecting the CRTC to develop a set of regulations, mimicking those already in telecommunication and broadcasting. The consultation process was uncharacteristically wide, with more than 1,000 individuals, interest groups and industry actors making submissions to the Commission. Across all the differences, all parties agreed that more clarity in the CRTC's approach to regulating the Internet was necessary. In its landmark decision in 1999 at the conclusion of the hearings and analysis, the Commission noted that as much of the Internet's content was alphanumeric text, it fell outside the scope of the *Broadcasting Act*. It declined to regulate that content. Other content such as audio, video or other visual images did fall within the definition of broadcasting; however, the CRTC felt that to regulate new media would

---

[44] CRTC (Ottawa: 19 May 1995).

not contribute to the policy goals of the pertinent legislation, nor would it support the important economic growth which the Internet was capable of supporting. Further, the Commission felt that, unlike other cultural industries in Canada, no additional economic incentives appeared to be necessary to stimulate a Canadian presence on the Internet — the market seemed to be providing the necessary conditions of possibility. Finally, the Commission felt that the Internet did not currently pose a competitive threat to the traditional media, but rather, was complementary to them. This meant that the CRTC did not need to regulate competition between the various media actors in new media and the exemption order was passed in December 1999.

Shortly after this, an incident challenged the hands-off approach the CRTC had taken. iCraveTV.com was a Canadian webcaster redistributing American television signals; it was picking them up through an antenna and retransmitting them on the Internet. They relied on the retransmission exception in the *Copyright Act*,[45] the same provision relied upon by cable operators when they redistribute content. A key difference however, was that iCraveTV.com had not paid the tariff that cable distributors do. This made the cable operators in Canada unhappy as well as American content producers asserting breach of copyright. Additionally, because the content was retransmitted on the Internet, Americans could view it for free. This made American broadcasters unhappy too. iCraveTV.com was sued by all of those groups and eventually, to avoid a heavy financial judgement and because they did not have the technological means to block U.S. viewers from receiving the content, they ultimately shut down. However, the irony should not be lost, that industry actors who had not wanted the CRTC to regulate the playing field of Internet supported media, suddenly wanted regulatory support against a web-based upstart.

The ensuing years have been consumed with the CRTC dealing with the implications of, and demands for exceptions to, its policy of non-intervention. In 2006 in a document entitled, "The Future Environment Facing the Canadian Broadcasting System", the CRTC again confirmed that it did not intend to regulate the Internet and that its approach of letting market conditions and competition govern new media development remained the preferable approach. This is consistent with the CRTC's trend towards more competition and less regulation and a continuing recognition that the Internet is a dramatically different form of medium, or set of media.

Most recently, in 2007, the CRTC initiated its New Media Project Initiative to further reflect on issues in new media broadcasting. In the

---

[45] R.S.C. 1985, c. C-42.

hearing process, a split emerged between telecommunications carriers, broadcasters and industry groups who, for the most part, were arguing that the CRTC's 1999 decision to stay out of Internet regulation was the right one. On the other hand, creators' groups and the CBC, for example, wanted more efforts to ensure access to, and production of, Canadian content, preferring similar regulations to those in the traditional broad-casting arena. In early June 2009, the CRTC released its new media decision, which largely repeated its previous and ongoing position. For the moment the CRTC has signalled that it does not want to, and will resist, forms of regulation of new media parallel to either broadcasting or telecommunications. It has preferred the logic of deregulated global competitiveness.

III. CONCLUSION

Freedom of expression is a right fundamental to Canadian society and its citizens. As the Supreme Court of Canada noted in *Edmonton Journal v. Alberta (Attorney General)*:

> It is difficult to imagine a guaranteed right more important to a democratic society than freedom of expression. Indeed a democracy cannot exist without that freedom to express new ideas and to put forward opinions about the functioning of public institutions. The concept of free and uninhibited speech permeates all truly democratic societies and institutions. The vital importance of the concept cannot be over-emphasized. No doubt that was the reason why the framers of the *Charter* set forth s. 2(*b*) in absolute terms which distinguishes it, for example, from s. 8 of the *Charter* which guarantees the qualified right to be secure from unreasonable search. It seems that the rights enshrined in s. 2(*b*) should therefore only be restricted in the clearest of circumstances.[46]

However, this is not the end of the story. There is an elaborate set of regulatory and legal mechanisms in place to administer the communi-cation and media arenas and a number of these have an impact, some directly, others more indirectly, on our abilities to freely express ourselves.

Some of these mechanisms are designed to stimulate industry, others to ensure Canadian ownership, manage limited resources, and still others to shape content. These policies all rely upon different underlying logics: those of cultural nationalism, technological sovereignty and deregulated

---

[46] [1989] S.C.J. No. 124, [1989] 2 S.C.R. 1326 at 1336 (S.C.C.).

global competitiveness. While there has been a slow and inexorable move towards deregulation and competition, Canada's quest for national identity through technological infrastructure and domestic content also persists.

Traditional distinctions that have long structured the communications regulatory domain are being challenged by convergence, both technological and cultural. We are in a moment of social change and it will be very interesting to see how the regulatory framework is adjusted to address this. Whatever the changes, they will continue to have significant impacts upon the means through which we communicate, the information we receive and the shape of our mass and personal mediascapes.

Chapter 2

Expression in the Public Interest:
Journalists and the Law

I. INTRODUCTION

Robert Picton, British Columbia's notorious serial killer, was charged with the first degree murder of 15 Vancouver women. A statutory publication ban was put in place for his preliminary hearing, preventing any journalist in Canada from publishing details of the evidence presented there. Picton wanted more; he requested that all journalists and spectators be banned from the hearing in order to prevent American journalists from publishing the evidence on the Internet. The court refused, but after one media organization published the entire opening day's evidence on its website, the judge made it clear that publication on the Internet was also banned. In no uncertain terms, he informed three American journalists that they would be excluded from the courtroom, and potentially charged, if the publications continued. They did not. Then again in 2005, when pre-trial hearings were under way, the court added to its publication ban that Canadian media should refrain from publishing or broadcasting any information that would lead readers or viewers to any other source where evidence was posted, namely foreign websites, blogs, *etc.*, and further that the media would be in violation of the ban if they created any hypertext links to such sites.

In January 2004 the RCMP raided *Ottawa Citizen* journalist, Juliet O'Neill's, home and office looking for information that might help them to identify an anonymous source from whom she had received a "leaked national security document". The alleged document pertained to the Canadian government's case against Syrian-born Canadian Maher Arar who had been arrested by U.S. officials and deported to Syria where he was tortured. O'Neill refused to reveal her source. Acting under the authority of the post-9-11 *Security of Information Act*,[1] the RCMP alleged that she had committed a criminal offence and obtained the search warrants; in addition they threatened her with criminal charges if

---
[1] R.S.C. 1985, c. O-5.

she did not cooperate. The Ontario Court of Justice not only quashed the warrants and reprimanded the RCMP for their heavy-handed behaviour, but also struck down section 4 of the *Security of Information Act* as a violation of the right of freedom of expression. It was too vague and overbroad to be constitutional. The judge held: "[t]his is legislation that fails to define in any way the scope of what it protects and then, using the most extreme form of government control, criminalizes the conduct of those who communicate and receive information that falls within its unlimited scope including the conduct of government officials and members of the public and of the press."[2] The Court recognized the primary relationship between confidentiality and freedom of expression:

> ... the spectre of law enforcement officials being able, by virtue of the leakage provisions of the SOIA, to threaten criminal charges so as to uncover a reporter's confidential source and thereby effect a "chill", even unintended, on the right of freedom of expression and of the press ... undermines the integrity of the judicial process.[3]

In October 1999 well-known British Columbia political commentator, Rafe Mair, wrote an editorial critical of the anti-homosexuality rhetoric of social activist, Kari Simpson. He suggested that her speech at a parents' meeting on the use of gay positive materials in public schools made him think of Governor Wallace in the United States shouting at crowds to keep African Americans out of Alabama schools. Simpson sued for defamation. In 2008, the Supreme Court of Canada, reinvigorating what is known as the fair comment defence, held: "Of course, 'chilling' false and defamatory speech is not a bad thing in itself, but chilling debate on matters of legitimate public interest raises issues of inappropriate censorship and self-censorship. Public controversy can be a rough trade, and the law needs to accommodate its requirements."[4] The Court found that Mair had not defamed Simpson in any way.

These three examples demonstrate the frequency with which journalists fall, or are accused of falling, afoul of the law. Most often, these laws are limits on freedom of expression that affect all of us. However, as we shall see throughout this chapter, journalists often operate as bellweathers of the boundaries of free expression in relation to other important social values. Some of the values that arise when journalists chafe against legal limits on expression include: the public interest in being informed about public affairs, the rights of those accused of crimes to receive fair trials, the protection of the privacy of the vulnerable, and

---

[2] *O'Neill v. Canada (Attorney General)*, [2006] O.J. No. 4189, 82 O.R. (3d) 241 at para. 62 (Ont. S.C.J.).
[3] *Ibid.*, at para. 159.
[4] *WIC Radio Ltd. v. Simpson*, [2008] S.C.J. No. 41, 2008 SCC 40 at para. 15 (S.C.C.).

the proper administration of justice. Journalists have no special status before the law and have only the same freedom of expression as other citizens. The inclusion in section 2(b) of the *Charter*[5] of "freedom of the press and other media of communication" is merely an example of the broader right of expression to which "everyone" is entitled. That said, however, courts have repeatedly recognized that the media play a key role in the way that we all mobilize our rights of freedom of expression. The Supreme Court of Canada said in a 1991 case, "[i]t is the media that, by gathering and disseminating news, enable members of our society to make an informed assessment of the issues which may significantly affect their lives and well-being."[6] As a result, not surprisingly, journalists and media organizations have been at the forefront of litigating many of the cases that have helped to define the parameters of freedom of expression in Canada.

There was a time, not long ago, when the legal environment of restraints on journalists' expression were strict and difficult to navigate. It was difficult for a reporter, editor or publisher to know where the boundaries between good journalism and contempt or defamation lay. That situation appears to be changing. There is a growing trend in recent case law of courts embracing the impacts of our highly mediated society and, as a result, beginning to loosen some of the strictures under which media have traditionally operated. Legal support for journalists is being enlivened when they are acting in the public interest. The balance is shifting away from the inevitable presumption of the prevalence of legal rights in relation to the administration of justice over freedom of expression. A more balanced approach is being sought. Arguably freedom of expression is currently in ascendancy with respect to the encounter between journalists and the law.

II. PUBLICATION BANS

Media are one of the key mechanisms through which citizens learn about the law and the legal system. Rarely does the average person go downtown to attend a criminal trial or go online to read about the latest legislative amendments being proposed in Parliament. Through news reports we learn about the legal system and develop our broader notions of how the law works. Journalists' access to the courts and the legal limits placed on it, therefore form a significant area of law impacting

---

[5] Part I of *The Constitution Act*, being Schedule B to the *Canada Act 1982* (U.K.), 1982, c. 11.
[6] *CBC v. New Brunswick (Attorney-General)*, [1991] S.C.J. No. 88, [1991] 3 S.C.R. 459 at 475 (S.C.C.).

upon the media's capacity to exercise its freedom of expression and to facilitate ours to be informed.

Courts in Canada are subject to what is known as the "principle of openness", namely that the courts are public institutions and the business that transpires within them is public business. For this reason, citizens should be, and generally are, entitled to attend any court proceeding. This includes journalists. Open courts are considered to be one of the pillars of a democratic society where only law, transparently rendered, can be just. Justice Estey of the Supreme Court of Canada described the principle in these terms:

> [t]he governing principles of access by the public to the courtroom are based upon the theory that public surveillance of the components of the judicial system performing in the courtroom keeps the process intellectually honest, and at the same time contributes to the need for the efficiency of the judicial process. Most importantly of all, however, open access to a public trial ensures that the outcome of the trial will be just.[7]

As most of us do not have the time or inclination to attend court proceedings on a regular basis, the media serve as our "proxy". They keep us informed about trials and court processes that are relevant to all of us and raise issues of broader concern. They serve therefore, a dual role as both "informer" and "watchdog".[8] The courts have recognized that while journalists do not have any special rights under the *Charter* not available to any other citizen, they do, in practice, play a special role:

> [t]he open court principle is inextricably linked to the freedom of expression protected by s. 2(b) of the *Charter* and advances the core values therein ... The freedom of the press to report on judicial proceedings is a core value. Equally, the right of the public to receive information is also protected by the constitutional guarantee of freedom of expression ... The press plays a vital role in being the conduit through which the public receives that information regarding the operation of public institutions. ... Consequently, the open court principle, to put it mildly, is not to be lightly interfered with.[9]

However, just as the right of freedom of expression is not absolute, neither is our right of open access to the courts. Openness often gives way

---

[7]   Estey, Willard Z. "Freedom of Expression vs. The Individual's Right to Privacy" in Frederic L.R. Jackman, ed. *Media & Society* (Toronto: The Canadian Journalism Foundation and the Empire Club of Canada, 1994) 27-41 at 39.

[8]   Jobb, Dean. *Media Law for Canadian Journalists* (Toronto: Emond Montgomery Publications, 2006) at 74.

[9]   *Vancouver Sun (Re)*, [2004] S.C.J. No. 41, [2004] 2 S.C.R. 332 at para. 26 (S.C.C.). See also *Edmonton Journal v. Alberta (Attorney-General)*, [1989] S.C.J. No. 124, [1989] 2 S.C.R. 1326 (S.C.C).

to other social interests such as the goals of the effective and efficient administration of justice, the privacy rights of victims and witnesses, and the right of the accused to a fair trial, guaranteed in the *Charter* in section 11(d). Publication bans — or the prohibition of the publication or broadcast of prejudicial information about a pending or transpiring case — are one of the most common instances where the openness principles gives way and the media's freedom of expression is directly constrained. Part of the broader law of contempt, there are both discretionary publication bans that can be granted without specific legislative provision under the court's general authority to manage its proceedings and statutory publication bans (some mandatory, some discretionary), the conditions for which are specifically provided in federal and provincial legislation.

Publication bans necessarily restrict the freedom of expression of the media and violate the principle of openness as they prohibit journalists from publishing information that would otherwise be public. Usually the ban is a delay of publication, rather than an outright prohibition; however, in the current news environment, "old" news is often no longer publishable. Most publication bans cease to exist once the trial resolves in some way, namely, a verdict is announced, the accused pleads guilty or the charges are dismissed. In general, to obtain a publication ban, the party arguing for it must demonstrate that there is an important objective to be achieved, it has to be limited in scope, it needs to be limited in time and be specific in relation to the content constrained. The judge hearing the application is also obliged to consider other means by which the same objective might be achieved.

Numerous benefits are claimed for publication bans in certain instances, including: preventing a jury from being influenced by information other than that presented in evidence during the trial; maximizing the chances that witnesses will testify because they will not be fearful of the consequences of publicity; protecting vulnerable witnesses (*e.g.,* children, police informants, victims of sexual offences); preserving the privacy of individuals involved in the criminal process; maximizing the chances of rehabilitation for young offenders; encouraging the reporting of sexual offences; saving the financial and/or emotional costs to the state, accused, victims and witnesses of the alternatives to publication bans (*e.g.,* delaying trials, changing venues, *etc.*); and even protecting national security. On the other hand, keeping the process open can maximize the chances of individuals with relevant information hearing about a case and coming forward with new information; prevent perjury by placing witnesses under public scrutiny; protect against state and/or court wrongdoing by placing the criminal justice process under public scrutiny; reduce crime through the public display of disapproval of crime; and promote the discussion of important issues in civil society.

A. Discretionary Bans

The test in Canada for a discretionary publication ban was stated emphatically by the court in the *Dagenais* case.[10] There, the CBC, with the National Film Board, had produced a docu-drama entitled, *The Boys of St. Vincent*, exploring the issues behind the sexual abuse charges laid against several Christian Brothers who ran the Catholic Mount Cashel orphanage in Newfoundland. The trial of one of the brothers charged with child sexual abuse was taking place at the time and the film was going to air on CBC just before the jury in the case was to make its decision. The Ontario Court of Justice awarded an injunction, or court order prohibiting the broadcast, without even notifying the CBC. The CBC, not surprisingly, appealed to the Ontario Court of Appeal, which upheld the injunction but limited its effect to Ontario and one television station in Montreal. The CBC again appealed, this time to the Supreme Court of Canada.

That Court quashed the ban and held that the accused's right to a fair trial should not automatically trump the media's right to freedom of expression. There is no hierarchy of rights; all rights have equal status and must be weighed in each instance. The Court set out the test for a discretionary publication ban. A publication ban should only be ordered when first, the ban is necessary in order to prevent a real risk to the fairness of the trial and other reasonable alternatives will not prevent that risk, and second, the positive effects of the ban outweigh the negative impacts upon freedom of expression.[11] The Court made it very clear that such bans should be the exception and not the norm.

Often discretionary publication bans are sought in instances where there are separate trials for co-defendants as the defendant being tried later in time is concerned that they will be negatively affected by the publicity from the first trial. This does not result in the restriction of all news from the first trial, merely the withholding of the name of the co-defendant and any evidence pertaining to their possible guilt. For example, there were publication bans in place at Karla Homolka's sentencing hearing after she pled guilty to manslaughter charges that were ordered to protect the fair trial rights of her co-accused, Paul Bernardo.

Very rarely will courts use publication bans to engage in the prior restraint of media, or the restriction of the publication of information associated with the defendant before the trial begins. But it does happen. For example, the Saskatchewan courts barred CTV from broadcasting a

---

10 *Dagenais v. Canadian Broadcasting Corp.*, [1994] S.C.J. No. 104, [1994] 3 S.C.R. 835 (S.C.C.).
11 *Ibid.*, at 878.

film about the David Milgaard story because they were concerned about protecting the fairness of the trial of Larry Fisher who was eventually convicted of the murder of Gail Miller. This was an unusual situation, however, as Milgaard had previously been (wrongly) convicted of the same crime and had gone to jail for 23 years. The Saskatchewan legal system had taken a beating in the eyes of the public for its conduct of those proceedings and was very interested in ensuring Fisher's trial was not tainted in any way.

B. Statutory Bans

Statutory publication bans were first introduced in the 1950s to protect the rights of those accused of crimes to a fair trial. During the 1980s, largely as the result of political lobbying by women's groups, victim's groups and youth advocates, the principle of nonpublicity was extended to protect the identities of complainants and young witnesses in sexual offence cases. A number of other limits have been added or existing ones revised since that time. Generally, statutory publication bans exist to protect the vulnerable. The most commonly invoked are those involving the criminal proceedings preceding a trial, those involving young persons in criminal trials, those protecting complainants and witnesses in sexual offence trials, and those protecting the vulnerable more broadly in criminal trials. The court does not have the same kind of discretion that it does at common law if the ban in the legislation is mandatory. The *Dagenais* test does not apply and the court's hands are tied: it must order the ban.

Certain kinds of court proceedings have different rules of procedure and evidence than do trials and so there are limitations on publishing details of evidence from these proceedings as they may ultimately be held inadmissible at trial. The assumption behind this is either that these cases are being heard by juries whose members may be negatively influenced by having knowledge of this additional information or that the accused will be "tried by the media". Publication bans are mandatory at bail hearings, where the parties make submissions to the judge about whether or not the accused can be released pending trial or should remain in custody, and at preliminary hearings which are held in serious criminal cases in order to ensure that there is sufficient evidence to warrant a full trial. In either of these instances, the court must grant the ban if the accused so requests. However, the section of the *Criminal Code*[12] pertaining to bail hearings has been successfully challenged in Alberta

---

[12] R.S.C. 1985, c. C-46.

on constitutional grounds.[13] The Alberta Court of Appeal, in a split decision, held that section 517 should be "read down" to comply with the *Charter* guarantee of freedom of expression. It should only apply to jury trials and only when requested by the accused; the dissenting judges would have eliminated the mandatory ban altogether. An appeal is pending to the Supreme Court of Canada. It would seem that the assumptions behind mandatory publication bans may be under challenge as an undue limit on freedom of expression.

There are various legal contexts where journalists are prevented from reporting the identity (or information leading to the identification) of those under the age of majority who are involved in some manner in a criminal proceeding. The federal *Youth Criminal Justice Act*,[14] for example, provides for bans on identifying young persons charged with a crime, as well as victims or witnesses. If the accused requests the ban, then the judge must grant it, but if the accused does not do so, then the decision rests with the trial judge. The public can still be in the courtroom and journalists are still permitted to take notes for future publications (books, articles and so on for release after the trial's conclusion). Unlike other publication bans, those preventing the identification of a young person are permanent. The rationale for this limitation is that it protects the privacy of victims and complainants and contributes to a context of rehabilitation for the alleged offender. Exceptions exist if the accused is being tried as an adult, if they consent to their identification once they turn 18 years of age, or if the identification will lead to finding other suspects in the crime. These exceptions have been endorsed by the courts.[15] There are also permanent limitations on reporting the identity of victims and witnesses who are minors involved in certain serious sex-related offences provided for in the *Criminal Code*. Again, Alberta courts are challenging the constitutionality of mandatory press bans, this time those protecting victims. In a 2001 case, the Alberta Court of Queen's Bench found the ban an unjustified violation of freedom of expression.[16]

There are laws to protect other parties in the criminal justice system who are assumed to be vulnerable. Over the 1980s and 1990s, debates arose about what came to be known as "the rape shield law" in Canada. Authorities had realized that sex-related crimes such as rape, were significantly under-reported by victims. It was felt that part of the reason for the reticence of victims to come forward and testify against

---

[13] *R. v. White*, [2007] A.J. No. 608, 2007 ABQB 359, 420 A.R. 1 (Alta. Q.B.), revd [2008] A.J. No. 956, 2008 ABCA 294, 298 D.L.R. (4th) 659 (Alta. C.A.).
[14] S.C. 2002, c. 1.
[15] *Re CBC and Halifax Herald Ltd.*, [2006] N.S.J. No. 226, 244 N.S.R. (2d) 90 (N.S. Prov. Ct.).
[16] *R. v. Thomson*, [2001] A.J. No. 1544, 2001 ABQB 962 (Alta. Q.B.).

their assailants was that their own history of sexual conduct and mental health would, under the guise of the examination of credibility, be open to public scrutiny. The victim would be under attack both in the courtroom and in the media. There are now provisions in the *Criminal Code* which prohibit the publication of the identity of sexual offence victims and young witnesses in sexual offence proceedings. As well, sections 276.2 and 276.3 restrict the publication of proceedings to determine the admissibility of evidence regarding a sexual assault complainant's sexual history and there are further limits on the publication of information from confidential records pertaining to the victim.

Similar protection to that provided to minors was extended in 1999 to all witnesses and victims. These *Criminal Code* provisions allow any witness or victim to request a ban on the publication of their identity or of any information that could lead to their identification. These provisions were enacted in order to encourage the reporting of crimes by victims and are granted primarily for those witnesses or victims who would be made particularly vulnerable by testifying in a trial and subject to retaliation. Examples include: informants, prison inmates, politicians, undercover police officers, people whose sexual identity would be revealed, and so on. In determining if the publication ban should be awarded to protect a vulnerable participant in a legal proceeding, the court must weigh the risk to the person's safety against freedom of expression of the media and the principle of openness.

Other evidence that must be treated with caution by journalists includes confidential records, such as medical, psychiatric, counselling, education and employment records, journals and diaries, adoption and social service records. There are also an array of other statutory publication bans pertaining to election results and polls; extradition proceedings; immigration hearings; national security, defence and sensitive government information; Canadian judicial inquiries; military courts martial; and some administrative tribunals. Many provinces provide for publication bans in relation to child protection cases; fatality inquiries; judicial council inquiries; discovery hearings for members of professionals; and for some tribunals and public inquiries.

C. The Internet and Publication Bans

Regardless of whether a publication ban is discretionary or statutory, the Internet poses a substantial challenge to its effectiveness and enforceability. This fact has not been lost on courts in Canada, although they seem somewhat at a loss in how to deal with it. In the *Dagenais* decision, the court recognized that the Internet creates "considerable difficulties for those who seek to enforce bans. ... In this global electronic age, meaningfully restricting the flow of information is becoming increasingly difficult."[17] During the Karla Homolka sentencing hearing, a number of publication bans were put into place to protect the victims of the crimes, but also to protect the right of her co-accused Paul Bernardo to receive a fair trial. It quickly became apparent that the media environment, the close proximity of the American press and the early Internet, rendered this ban of limited effectiveness. Because the court has no jurisdiction to enforce a contempt judgement on an American journalist or media outlet, media in the United States could circulate all the lurid and horrifying details of the murders. At one point, the court prevented foreign journalists from entering the courtroom, given that a number of American media outlets had already announced their intentions to violate the broad publication ban. What resulted was a rush by the Canadian public to obtain news of the trial from elsewhere. An overnight cross-border traffic in American and British newspapers developed. Illegal satellite reception of American tabloid news programs took off and interest groups formed on the Internet. Even libraries were caught up in the action, serving as havens for those wanting to read news of the Canadian proceeding in newspapers from other jurisdictions. In light of what happened in the Homolka case, courts must weigh the impact on the public perception of the legal system if ineffective and unenforceable bans are put into place that are subsequently disrespected by the media and the public.

This may have been what caused Justice Gomery to discontinue the publication ban he originally ordered on the testimony of three key witnesses in the inquiry bearing his name into the Liberal government sponsorship scandal. It was not long before the content of that testimony was circulating on the "blogosphere" and the ban could not be enforced. Amateur journalists were going where professional journalists, more vulnerable to contempt proceedings, were not willing/able to go. There was also considerable criticism of the publication ban in this particular proceeding, which was supposed to be a public hearing into government misdeeds — seemingly one of the very reasons why media are permitted to be in such proceedings in the first place. In this case, the bans were removed.

While there may be sound public policy reasons for publication bans, if journalists and citizens really want to circulate the particular information, they can do so. Nothing short of closing the doors of the courtroom is going to stop those who are determined to break the ban, and as we saw with the Gomery Inquiry and the Homolka hearing, these are most often going to be amateur journalists, pundit citizens and non-Canadian

---

[17] *Dagenais*, at para. 89.

journalists. Thus, the technology of the Internet, facilitated by an ethos of the free circulation of information, is increasingly trumping the rights of the accused and the vulnerable in relation to the issue of publicity. While the courts and legislatures will continue to engage in the balancing of freedom of expression against these other social values, not everyone will. Whether or not this will result, in Canada, in the legal-media spectacles that have occurred around certain cases in the United States seems unlikely however, given our less extensive culture of celebrity, differing news values and different political cultures.

III. CONFIDENTIALITY OF SOURCES

The second major context in which journalists invoke freedom of expression to defend their professional practices is in their clashes with the law about the confidentiality of sources and the revealing of confidential information received from a source. These disputes, too, like publication bans, are treated under the law of contempt. And again, like the area of publication bans, in the past, the common law of contempt has been uncertain, complex and not kindly disposed to journalists' claims for confidentiality. While individual judges were often sensitive to the reporters' work, the provisions within the common law itself were not generally supportive of the media. However, increasingly in recent years it seems that courts are aware of the negative impact that contempt law has had on the journalist-confidential source relationship, and again we see the balance shifting towards greater support for freedom of expression.

Much of the work of the investigative journalist is in tracking down information that is not widely available. Often sources will only want to speak to a journalist if they can be given some kind of reassurance that their identity will not be revealed in the resulting article or broadcast. They ask for this confidentiality because they fear the negative consequences that will result from someone in a position of power over them learning that they provided the information. This is a very legitimate concern and one which journalists have historically worked very hard to protect. As well, sometimes sources provide information or documents to a journalist which they probably should not — *i.e.*, they "leak" the information. However, sometimes the source feels the greater good will be served by that information becoming public and are willing to face the risk of its disclosure. However, the journalist does not want to become a means by which law enforcement officials like police and prosecutors obtain evidence. Many analysts and journalists assert that to make the journalist part of the legal process by requiring her to be a witness and reveal her documents or by requiring him to reveal his sources, will have what is called a "chilling effect" on their practice. The chilling effect means that the journalist, herself, will be less willing to report certain stories, but also that sources will be much less willing to talk to journalists if they do not have a reasonable expectation of confidentiality. Unlike other professionals who have historically been able to claim that their communications were privileged, such as lawyers or priests, journalists do not have any specific privilege recognized by the law.

In general there are four criteria that are typically deployed by Canadian courts to determine whether or not a relationship is confidential and should be respected by the law. They are collectively referred to as the Wigmore Test, and American courts follow it as well.[18] First, the communication must have originated in the confidence that it would not be disclosed. Second, the relationship between the parties must be such that confidentiality goes to the heart of it. Third, the confidential relationship must be of a sort that is valued by the community and should be supported; and fourth, the damage that would be suffered to the confidential relationship through the disclosure of the communication must be greater than the benefit to be gained in relation to the disposition of the legal case before the court. Courts in Canada have held that journalists could make a claim for privilege under the Wigmore criteria, but until recently in Canada, most courts had found that the relationship between a journalist and his or her source did not meet the fourth requirement.

However, in *R. v. National Post*, the Ontario Superior Court broke new ground, holding that journalists have a legal right pursuant to section 2(b) of the *Charter* to protect the identities of their sources.[19] The case involved the reporter who broke the "Shawinigate" story — namely the allegations of conflict of interest of then Prime Minister Jean Chrétien in relation to a loan to an inn in his home town and in which his family held an interest. The Court was clearly concerned that the sources revealing such misbehaviours might "dry up" if they were not confident that their identities would be protected. The judge wrote that confidential sources are "essential to the effective functioning of the media in a free and democratic society".[20] She went on:

> It is through confidential sources that matters of great public importance are made known. As corporate and public power increase, the ability of the average citizen to affect his or her world depends upon the information disseminated by the press. To deprive the media of an

---

18 Wigmore, John Henry. *Evidence in Trials at Common Law*, McNaughton Revision, vol. 8, (Boston: Little Brown & Co, 1961).
19 [2004] O.J. No. 178, 69 O.R. (3d) 427 (Ont. S.C.J.), revd [2008] O.J. No. 744, 89 O.R. (3d) 1 (Ont. C.A.).
20 *Ibid.*

important tool in the gathering of news would affect society as a whole.[21]

The case was overturned on appeal, however, based upon its facts. Because the document at issue was alleged to have been a forgery, in refusing to reveal the source, the journalist may have been inadvertently covering up another crime, namely a conspiracy against a Prime Minister. The need to pursue that investigation was found to outweigh the claim of privilege. The Ontario Court of Appeal did not deny the claim of privilege, but noted that while in pursuit of their constitutionally guaranteed right to produce news, journalists are entitled to protect their sources, that protection loses much of its value when it is being used to protect the identity of a potential criminal or to conceal possible evidence of a crime. Leave to appeal the case to the Supreme Court of Canada has been granted and the case was heard as part of a series of cases on the issue. We await the decisions.

Another recent and important case supported the journalist in his protection of a source. Journalist Ken Peters had been found in contempt of court for failing to answer the question: "Who is B?" as it would have revealed the identity of a confidential source. The Ontario Court of Appeal allowed the appeal, setting aside his contempt conviction. The decision is an important one for journalists and lays out a number of key principles. First, the court recognizes the importance of the work that journalists do to the functioning of democratic society. Second, it recognizes the value of confidential sources to journalists and states that this relationship does not have to be proved with empirical evidence for the court to so note it. Third, the court states that the application of the Wigmore test and the analysis of privilege should be conducted keeping in mind the values of the *Charter* guarantee of freedom of expression. "Freedom of expression and freedom of the media, protected by s. 2(b) of the *Charter*, have a direct bearing on a journalist's claim to confidentiality."[22] A contempt citation for a journalist should, as a result, be the court's very last resort. Interestingly, the source's identity did not remain confidential at the end of the day because the pressure that had been placed on the journalist led to him revealing his own identity.[23]

If a journalist has information about events pertinent to a case or is a material witness, then he or she may be required to testify just as any other citizen would be. However, courts have also been sensitive to the chilling effect that requiring journalists to testify when not entirely

---

[21] *Ibid.*

[22] *St. Elizabeth Home Society v. Hamilton (City)*, [2008] O.J. No. 983, 2008 ONCA 182 at para. 27 (Ont. C.A.).

[23] This case has not been appealed to the Supreme Court.

necessary would have, and of letting lawyers go on "fishing expedi-
tions".[24] The Supreme Court of British Columbia set out a three-part test
for when a journalist may be required to testify. First, the journalist's
evidence must relevant to the case. Second, there must be no other viable
means through which the same evidence might be obtained; and third,
the court must balance the impact of the evidence on the case with the
negative effect of such an order on the media's capacity to do their job.[25]

In relaxing the fourth requirement of the Wigmore test and in the
embrace of the *Charter* values associated with freedom of expression
in its application, the courts seem to be signalling that they are
more prepared than ever to respect the relationship between the journalist and her source. While the court will still continue to weigh the
competing interests, the balance seems to have shifted slightly towards
the journalists. That said, commentators still counsel journalists to tell
their sources that they cannot guarantee complete confidentiality, but will
do everything they can to ensure that their identity is not revealed.

IV. DEFAMATION

The third major area of law that shapes the free expression of journalists
and thus of us, as citizens, is that of defamation. Print and broadcast
media have historically had the right to comment upon, criticize, and
engage with the actions of others, particularly those involved in public
affairs, politicians or judges, for example. However, this right, like all
other modes of expression, is not unlimited and the art of criticism of
public figures is a delicate one. Defamation law pits the right of one
person's freedom of expression against the right of another person to
his reputation. Defamation is, therefore, one of the limits of which
journalists must be aware when writing about others, and it too has
been recognized by courts as having a potentially chilling effect on
journalism.[26]

A statement is defamatory if it meets the following test: would the
communication tend to lower the aggrieved individual in the estimation
of right-thinking members of society generally? Therefore, statements
that impugn the honesty or integrity of an individual can be defamatory.
A mere insult or something derogatory may not be enough to constitute
defamation, rather the statement must lower the person in the eyes of
others, not merely offend the person who is its subject. However, falsely

---

[24] See, for example, *R. v. Baltovich*, [2004] O.J. No. 4880, 73 O.R. (3d) 481 (Ont. C.A.).
[25] *R. v. Hughes*, [1988] B.C.J. No. 1694 (B.C.S.C.).
[26] *Cusson v. Quan*, [2007] O.J. No. 4348, 87 O.R. (3d) 241 (Ont. C.A.).

alleging that someone is a criminal, is racist, is dishonest, is involved in a conflict of interest, is corrupt, has engaged in sexual misbehaviour and so on, are all statements likely to be potentially defamatory. It is interesting to reflect on how language that impacts upon a person's reputation changes over time. For example, the pianist Liberace won a defamation action against a British newspaper in the late 1950s because they suggested he was a homosexual. The allegation of being gay, while potentially problematic for the individual in question, would be much less likely to be found to damage one's reputation today. In other words, what constitutes defamation is historically contingent.

Defamation gives all of us rights in our reputation and its protection. Our reputation becomes an enforceable boundary that we can sue over if anyone damages it. Defamation law works on the assumption that a person being able to maintain her reputation is significant to the moral well-being of our society. As the Supreme Court of Canada stated, a good reputation,

> … enhances an individual's sense of worth and value. False allegations can so very quickly and completely destroy a good reputation. A reputation tarnished by libel can seldom regain its former lustre. A democratic society, therefore, has an interest in ensuring that its members can enjoy and protect their good reputation so long as it is merited.[27]

As Dean Jobb also points out, however, defamation law is an encouragement to good journalism as well. "Although defamation law imposes limits on free speech to protect the reputations of individuals, it also defends good journalism and the media's role as public informer and government critic."[28] He argues this is the case because news stories and commentary that are based on true facts and are balanced and fair will not be found to be defamatory, and should media organizations and individual journalists act professionally and responsibly, defamation cases should be rare.

Defamation historically includes both libel and slander. Libel is defamation with the written word or words in some permanent form, with permanent form having been interpreted to include publishing, broadcast, on computer discs, hard drives, audiotape, videotape and film. Slander is defamation with the spoken word or words in a non-permanent form. However, this distinction has largely fallen out of use and has been criticized as being no longer relevant. Defamation is governed in Canada by both common and statutory law. Jurisdiction over defamation rests

---

27 *Hill v. Church of Scientology of Toronto*, [1995] S.C.J. No. 64, [1995] 2 S.C.R. 1130 (S.C.C.).
28 Jobb, Dean. *Media Law for Canadian Journalists* (Toronto: Emond Montgomery Publications, 2006) at 265.

with the provinces and all of them except Quebec have legislation governing it; however, because the legislation tends to deal only with some aspects of defamation, the common law remains relevant.[29] As well, an offence of criminal libel does exist, but is rarely pursued and will not be treated here.

Defamation can be in words, visual presentation, or any type of expression and does not merely capture actual statements by the media organization, but also any meaning generated from any of the media content. So, in addition to photographs, articles, headlines and editorials, the layout of a page of a newspaper is relevant — it may be an issue whether a photograph from one article looks like it might be associated with the title of a different article. A television or radio news reader's suggestive tone of voice may be defamatory in combination with the words uttered. As well, content that is not even produced by the media organization such as news stories reproduced from a news agency, letters to the editor, classified advertisements and so on, are all relevant in considering whether or not the newspaper has defamed someone. However, at the same time, the comment cannot be understood in isolation, but will be viewed in the context of the entire article, segment of broadcast and so on.

Defamation is what is known as a "strict liability offence", meaning that even though the statement might have been made innocently without knowledge of its falsity, or the harm from it may have been unintended, the author or publisher may still be found liable, unless he or she has a defence. In other words, the intent to defame is irrelevant. What does this then do to the standard disclaimer at the end of every film that assures viewers that all the characters and events depicted in the film are fictitious and no reference to any person living or dead is intended? It renders it moot. It provides no protection against a claim of defamation if the other requirements are met. As well, it is not a defence for a media organization to argue that it was merely republishing something that someone else wrote — everyone who publishes a defamatory statement is responsible for it. Therefore, in the context of a newspaper, the author of the article, the editor of that section, the manager of the paper and the publisher of the paper could all be sued in relation to the same allegation of defamation.

In order to succeed with a defamation action, the complainant must demonstrate three things. First, the words must be shown to be defamatory in their ordinary and natural meaning or by innuendo. The words will be interpreted in the manner that they would be by a reasonable

---

[29] Quebec does have protections for reputation in its *Civil Code*, but they are quite different from the common law tradition.

person of ordinary intelligence and must be judged to be capable of harming their reputation. Second, the words must refer to the complainant. He or she does not have to be expressly named, but must be recognizable. The test for recognition is whether or not reasonable people would reasonably believe that this was the complainant. The person must be specifically recognizable, not merely a member of a group which is maligned. In a ground-breaking series reporting on institutional racism and racial profiling in the Toronto police, the *Toronto Star* was alleging racism against some members of the police force. However, according to the Ontario Court of Appeal, because individual officers were not named, there was no defamation action available.[30] The person must also be alive; because defamation is a personal right, the right to one's reputation dies with the person. As well, corporations, falling within the legal definition of person, can also sue for the defamation of their reputation. Courts in Canada have distinguished themselves from their American counterparts in preserving the rights of public figures to successfully pursue defamation actions. The famous have much less recourse in the United States; any allegations against a public figure in Canada must be anchored in truth. The third requirement of a successful defamation action is that the communication has to be published, namely, made known to people other than the complainant. Publication includes written communication, the display of signs or images, broadcasting and all other permanent or partially permanent ways of fixing text or image.

There are four primary defences to a defamation action: justification, privilege, fair comment and innocent dissemination. A defence of consent also exists, but is extremely rare in practice. Justification is the defence that the statement alleged to be defamatory is, in fact, a true statement. This is an absolute defence, even if the communication was published with malice. The rationale for this is that the law should not allow the person to recover damages for an injury to reputation for a reputation that he or she has not rightfully earned. In practice, this is a very difficult defence to successfully employ because it is extremely difficult to prove the truth of something and the court starts from the position that the statement is false. It can also be a dangerous defence because if it fails, the court is likely to award more damages to the complainant.

The existence of the defence of truth to a defamation claim sometimes results in interesting situations, however. In 1993, black teenager Stephen Lawrence was killed in south-east London, allegedly by a group of white youths in what appeared to be a racially motivated murder. Both police

---

[30] *Gauthier v. Toronto Star Daily Newspapers Ltd.*, [2003] O.J. No. 2622, 228 D.L.R. (4th) 748 (Ont. S.C.J.), affd [2004] O.J. No. 2686, 245 D.L.R. (4th) 169 (Ont. C.A.).

and prosecutors were accused of racism and misconduct in relation to the investigation of the case and the trials and acquittals of three of the accuseds. In 1997, the *Daily Mail* newspaper ran a provocative story covering its entire front page featuring the photographs of the five accused youth with a headline "Murderers!" in large black letters. The paper claimed that it believed that the five were guilty and added, "if we are wrong, let them sue us". Basically the paper was challenging the five young men to sue them for defamation. The paper's intention was to claim the defence of justification and to bring out, through a civil trial for defamation, the evidence and convictions that it felt had not been achieved in the criminal proceedings. While a defamation suit was never brought, the actions of the *Daily Mail* and their effect on public opinion did arguably play a role in the eventual official inquiry into the handling of the case that resulted in charges of incompetence and institutional racism against the police and a wealth of recommendations to the legal system in London.

The second defence available to the media is that of qualified privilege. As noted in the discussion of confidentiality of sources, the media are not generally subject to any automatic privilege, nor to absolute privilege. They can, however, claim a qualified privilege through their right to freedom of expression. The press does have absolute privilege when it is reporting on either parliamentary or court matters when it reports them fairly and accurately. Therefore, if one Member of Parliament slanders another in the House of Commons, CTV is able to broadcast that slander on the evening news, provided that it does so in the context of reporting on parliamentary affairs fairly and accurately, which in this case would mean providing a context for the discussion resulting in the slander.

The third defence is that of fair comment, and this is the defence most often claimed by the media (as well as by satirists, parodists and cartoonists). Obviously, fair comment is integral to both the media's freedom of expression, but also the public's right, in a democratic society, to find out what is going on with respect to matters of legitimate public interest. There are five requirements for a successful defence of fair comment. First, the comment has to be on a matter of public interest. The underlying assumption made here is that every citizen has the right to comment upon the actions of public figures or institutions that concern us as citizens. Matters of public interest include all public figures, matters of government, the justice system, literature and entertainment (such as reviews), as well as the conduct and content of the news media. A private individual may not be accepted as the subject matter of fair comment by the courts, given the focus of this defence upon public affairs. The test for whether or not a matter is in the public interest has been framed as: "[w]henever a matter is such as to affect people at large, so that they may be legitimately interested in, or concerned at, what is going on or what may happen to them or others; then it is a matter of public interest on which everyone is entitled to make fair comment."[31]

The second component to the defence of fair comment is that the comment must be fair, and by that is meant, it must be based upon true facts. A genuine mistake or a real belief in the truth of the facts underlying the comment will not stop the defence from failing if the facts turn out to be false. Third, for a finding of a defence of fair comment, the words in question have to be a comment on facts and not a statement of fact in itself. A comment is an inference made on the basis of a set of facts. The logic works this way: if all of the facts have been presented truthfully, then a comment cannot be libellous because it is related to the truth, and presumably the reader or listener could have drawn the same impression on her or his own anyway. Fourth, the comment should be the honest opinion of the person who makes it. If that individual is outside of the media organization, then provincial legislation tends to permit the defence of fair comment provided someone could reasonably hold that opinion. Fifth, the comment cannot be malicious.

The fourth defence of innocent dissemination applies when a party distributing a message does not know that it is defamatory, had no reason to suspect that it was, and took reasonable steps to avoid being used as a mechanism for the transmission of defamation. Historically, this defence has been relied upon by wholesalers, booksellers, news vendors, video stores and libraries who claim that they are mere distributors. The rationale is becoming familiar — that a mere conduit should not be held accountable for the substance of the content transmitted. Because Internet Service Providers ("ISPs") cannot be expected to monitor every message that passes through their facilities, they may well fall within the requirements necessary for the defence of innocent dissemination. Although the law on their status in relation to defamation in Canada is unclear, it would certainly be consistent with the ways in which ISPs are being understood more broadly within Canadian communication law. If an ISP is informed of a defamatory communication, however, it would likely have to take prompt and efficient action to have it removed in order to successfully avoid liability for defamation.

An apology is not a defence at common law to a defamation charge, but it remains very important nonetheless. Apologies can help to mitigate the damages that would otherwise be awarded for a successful claim. A well-done apology often causes the complainant to withdraw his or her claim because it may be interpreted as a vindication of his or her

---

[31] *London Artists v. Littler*, [1969] 2 Q.B. 375 at 391 (H.L.).

reputation. Numerous provincial statutes recognize apology or retraction as a means of reducing damages. To be successful, however, the apology should take place before the defamation action is launched (it appears too self-serving otherwise) and should be given the same prominence in that particular media form as was provided to the original defamatory statement. This means that if the original defamatory report ran on the first page of the newspaper or as the lead story on the nightly news, then the apology must do the same.

Defamation claims seem to be on the rise in Canada in recent years, and damage awards have been growing larger. Damages are typically related to the size of the audience who heard, read or saw the defamation, the nature of the defamatory claim, and the credibility of the media organization making the impugned statement. Because the size of the audience is relevant, publication online with the Internet's potentially huge audiences has dramatically impacted upon some damage awards. However, courts will expect to hear evidence of how many people did actually access a document and will not merely assume that the audience was millions of people, merely because it could have been.

There may be a new defence on the horizon, one emerging out of a recent Ontario Court of Appeal decision. The court recognized the trend towards opening up the defences to defamation claims in order to support and stimulate the free flow of information, and coined what it called the "public interest responsible journalism" defence. The court wanted to reject the common law approaches that unduly chill journalistic practice, but at the same time, not give a *carte blanche* to journalists to defame public figures at will. If a journalist publishes a story with every reason to believe that it is true, and the public has a legitimate interest in hearing it, then the journalist is protected even if some of the facts end up being incorrect. The requirement for truth is no longer absolute, but at the same time, the media organization must demonstrate that it took all reasonable steps to ensure the facts were true and that the story was fair. It will be interesting to see whether this test is adopted in other jurisdictions, but it is a clear condensation of the trends that seem to be at work in the shift in the balance towards freedom of expression in the area of defamation.

The Internet has posed some interesting challenges to the law of defamation and has meant that defamation is now more likely to be a relevant concern for the everyday person. Prior to this, non-journalists typically did not have much contact with defamation law because most of us did not publish information. The Internet has changed this with the rise of social networking sites and practices such as blogging, in particular. Key legal questions that have been raised before the courts in online defamation cases include the status of the ISP and the issue of jurisdiction. With its still slightly "wild-west" ethos, the Internet has served as an ideal media platform for ordinary individuals to engage in potentially defamatory speech. In particular, it has served as a forum for individuals upset with former employers and consumers angry with purveyors of goods and services. These specific practices have come to be known as "flaming", "cyberlibelling" and "cybersmearing". Courts have in fact recognized that the Internet is an extremely efficient medium through which to instantly, and potentially irrevocably, damage someone's reputation.

Courts have held that the fact that the Internet is being used for communication is irrelevant to whether or not the claim is published. As long as the information is made available to a third party, then regardless of whether it is contained in an email, on a website or in a blog, it is considered to have been published for the purposes of defamation law. The number of "hits" a particular website receives is irrelevant to the assessment of whether or not the comment was published, although it may be relevant as to damages. The crucial action is in making the defamatory comment available to a large number of people without restriction.[32] Other jurisdictions have suggested that even posting to access-limited forums such as Bulletin Board Systems ("BBSs") and listservs are still publication, in that the message will still be read by many others. Email is also considered a means of publication if the message is circulated to even one additional person. The author of the original defamatory message can even be held responsible for its subsequent retransmission if it was reasonably foreseeable that the message would be circulated more broadly.[33] Courts in Canada have recognized the power of email as a quick and easy tool of defamation, and have been hard on those who have deliberately used it for this purpose.[34] Posting anonymously does not resolve the issue as courts have been willing to require ISPs to provide identification information on their clients in order that they could be sued for defamation.

One of the ongoing vexing questions as the Internet begins to shape all forms of communications law is how ISPs should be treated. In general, as we have seen, and will see in Chapters 3 and 4 as well, most jurisdictions do not want to burden the ISP with too much liability for content, as they are the backbone of the rapid and efficient circulation of information between networks. The fear is that ISPs cannot do their jobs well if they are continually monitoring content and worried about being

---

[32] *Reform Party of Canada v. Western Union Insurance Co.*, [1999] B.C.J. No. 2794 (B.C.S.C.), revd [2001] B.C.J. No. 697 (B.C.C.A.).

[33] *Egerton v. Finucan*, [1995] O.J. No. 1653 (Ont. Gen. Div).

[34] See *Ross v. Holey*, 2004 CarswellOnt. 5093 (Ont. S.C.J.), where an Ontario man falsely accused an archaeologist of being a grave robber and emailed the message out to a large number of people. He was ordered to pay a substantial award of damages.

sued. However, the ISP is often the entity with the greater control over the flow of content, the holder of information about individual users and has greater financial resources than the average person. Courts in the United States have generally found that if the ISP does nothing to the content, exerts no editorial control, then it will not be held to be a publisher for the purposes of defamation law.[35] As well, provisions in the *Communications Decency Act* protect ISPs in the United States provided that they act only as a conduit and act responsibly.

The second ongoing issue produced by the intersection of the Internet and defamation law is that of jurisdiction — where exactly does the defamation take place? What is the place of publication? An early Canadian decision suggested that there must be a real and substantial connection between the location of the alleged defamation and the jurisdiction where the case is launched. Merely because someone might have read the defamation in some other location does not mean that the action can be brought there. The judge recognized the extremely negative effects on freedom of expression that would result if someone who posts something to the Internet could be liable to legal recourse from any corner of the world where the message could be read.[36] The rule of thumb that courts are using seems to be that the case should be heard in the jurisdiction where the damage to reputation occurs.

V. CONCLUSION

The line between who was a journalist and who was a consumer of the news used to be much clearer than it is now. With many people obtaining a significant portion of their news and information from sources other than the mainstream print and broadcast media, those once-easy distinctions become more murky. We are witnessing a certain democratization of the production, circulation, interpretation and consumption of information. I am not commenting on whether this is a positive or negative development but it will be interesting to see the effect it has, not only on established media outlets and journalistic expertise, but on the ways that we pursue the development of our rights of freedom of expression.

At the same time that citizens are becoming implicated in the maintenance and breach of publication bans and defamation claims, in particular, finding themselves in violation of the law more than in the past, this is not so with professional journalists. The somewhat notorious

---

[35] *Cubby v. Compuserve*, 776 F.Supp. 135 (S.D.N.Y.1991) and *Stratton Oakmount, Inc. v. Prodigy Services Company*, 23 Media L.R. 1794 (S.C. Nassau County 1995).

[36] In *Braintech Inc. v. Kostiuk*, [1999] B.C.J. No. 622, 171 D.L.R. (4th) 46 (B.C.C.A.).

lack of clarity and predictability of both contempt law (affecting both public bans and the confidentiality of sources) and defamation, is being recognized by the courts as negatively affecting the work of the professional journalist to an undue degree. We have seen the courts support, to a greater extent in recent years, the freedom of expression of the media and the right of the public to know.

Chapter 3

Propertizing Expression: Intellectual Property

I. INTRODUCTION

In 1996, the American Society of Composers, Authors and Publishers informed hundreds of children's summer camps that their campers could not sing their songs around the campfire without paying a licence fee of $1,200 per song. The makers of the film *Mad Hot Ballroom* had to pay $10,000 to EMI because a cell-phone rings in the background of one of the scenes and the ringtone is the theme from the film *Rocky*. Adobe's e-version of *Alice's Adventures in Wonderland* cannot be copied, read aloud or shared according to the user agreement that is a necessary condition of access, even though the original book can be. Donald Trump owns the phrase, "You're fired!", Verizon owns, "Can you hear me now?", Mastercard owns "Priceless", and Paris Hilton owns "That's hot!" All of these examples are instances where forms of human expression — songs, words and phrases, novels — have been turned into someone's property, and according to laws recognized around the world, those owners can limit and even prohibit others from accessing, consuming or using them. In Chapter 1 we recognized the crucial significance that expression plays in individual, social and political development and fulfillment. So, what happens when property and expression come together? The result is a form of property known as intellectual property.

While intellectual property rights have existed for hundreds of years to protect the rights of creators of cultural content, there are two key trends that mark the current experience of intellectual property as different from any other. First, we are seeing an increasingly rapid, and some would argue, rampant, move towards "propertization".[1] Increasingly, forms of expression that once would not have been subject to property claims at all or would have been considered public property shared by all of us, are being treated as the exclusive private property of individual

---

[1] I borrow this term from Carol M. Rose. "Romans, Roads and Romantic Creators: Traditions of Public Property in the Information Age" in (2003), 66 *Law and Contemporary Problems* 89 at 94.

owners. The second trend is that while more than at any other time in history, ordinary citizens are being affected by this rush to propertize, more importantly, they are aware of intellectual property laws and issues. Recent years have witnessed an explosion in the sense of ownership that consumers have over issues of copyright and trademark, in particular. This is yet another manifestation of the cultural convergence discussed in Chapter 1. Often this awareness is framed in claims to freedom of expression.

The current social field of intellectual property law is shaped by the push and pull of these two opposing social forces. The stakes of what forms of expression can be propertized, in what ways, by whom, and for how long, are high. As Edwin Hettinger notes, "[p]roperty institutions fundamentally shape a society."[2] And interestingly for the student of communication and law in a media society, these issues show no sign of being resolved any time soon. In the struggles that we are currently experiencing over the limits we want to place on the propertization of expression, we see a broader struggle over what the place of expression is in the kind of society we want to build.

This chapter takes up intellectual property issues, and more particularly those that arise out of copyright and trademark law as those domains have, in recent years, had the most dramatic impact upon the Canadian communication landscape. Intellectual property is one of three types of property, including: real property, or immovables, such as land or buildings; personal property, or movables, such as a pen or car; and intellectual property, or intangibles, the products of the mind, such as a painting or an invention. Intellectual property refers to the nonphysical property which stems from, is identified as, and whose value is based upon human ideas. Canada legally recognizes a number of forms of intellectual property: copyright, trademark, patent, trade secret, publicity law, industrial design, integrated circuit topography, and rights for plant breeders.

As with all forms of property, intellectual property can be usefully considered as a bundle of rights. While it is difficult to provide a universal definition, there are certain elements that all kinds of intellectual property share. All intellectual property carries with it some element of novelty or newness (although this is not absolute). Intellectual property rights do not accrue to ideas in the abstract, but only to those ideas as they have manifested in some tangible form. There are two kinds of ideas that are generally not subject to intellectual property rights: the common ones — the thought to wash one's car, or to go to class; and the important

2   Hettinger, Edwin C. "Justifying Intellectual Property" in John Haldane, ed., *Philosophy and Public Affairs* (New York: Cambridge University Press, 2001) at 31.

ones — like the Pythagorean theorem, the heliocentric theory of the solar system, or the arch. In a number of types of intellectual property there is an element of public interest in their constitution and administration and all forms of intellectual property make non-exclusive goods exclusive, with this exclusivity typically limited in time and scope.

Intellectual property is different from the other forms of property in a number of ways. For example, multiple consumers can use it at the same time. If I own my house, then no one else can own my house, be in my house or do anything to my house without affecting my real property rights in it. But millions of people can listen to Frank Sinatra's, "My Way" at the same time. Information is considered in property language to be a "non-rival good". It also means that use of intellectual property rights does not use up the property in the work to which the rights are attached. With continued use, eventually my car will break down and cease to be — this is not true of intellectual property rights. Intellectual property rights are also understood to be "non-excludable". I own the personal property in my copy of Michael Ondaatje's latest book and can stop my brother from reading it by physically taking the property away from him. However, not so with the intellectual property rights. Michael Ondaatje, because he does not own and cannot control the personal property I hold in his novel *Divisadero*, cannot easily exclude me from doing things with that book that will infringe the copyrights that he holds. Therefore, if I made (and therefore own) a recipe for a great new salad dressing, my ability to make and consume that salad dressing unhindered does not stop if someone else can also make the same salad dressing and use it on their salad. What this does affect, proponents of intellectual property rights would argue, is my ability to make maximum profits from selling my dressing in an open marketplace. And so a system has been developed to generate a set of legally enforceable rights for me to attempt to control the intangible rights that I have in that creation.

II. JUSTIFYING THE OWNERSHIP OF EXPRESSION

While it is one thing to provide intellectual property rights to a fiction writer or visual artist in order to aid them in making a living from their art, or to protect a company against false advertising from competitors, when Warner Brothers threatens to sue children making Harry Potter fan websites, when AOL/Time Warner polices the use of the song "Happy Birthday", when the Vancouver Olympic Committee applies to trademark "with glowing hearts", key words in the Canadian national anthem, or when Walt Disney Corporation enforces its trademarks in Hercules, Aladdin, Pocahontas, Cinderella and Snow White — stories that have existed for hundreds or even thousands of years — then intellectual property rights seem to be infringing upon freedom of expression. This may lead us to wonder: why do we protect intellectual property rights at all?

There are three common justifications offered for recognizing intellectual property: the labour justification, the personality justification, and the utilitarian or economic justification. The labour justification draws upon the work of political philosopher John Locke and suggests that a human who labours on raw material adds value to that thing and thus earns property rights in what they have made. Locke added two provisos to his basic proposition, namely that one had to leave enough resources for others in the future and one should not take any more property than one could use. Ultimately, Locke's justification for his labour theory of property is that one owns one's body. As my body is my property, when that body interacts with natural goods, they are transformed into products of my body, and can thus be also understood as my property. This theory has been related to human expression through the following reasoning. The production of ideas and the material expression of those ideas requires a person's labour. These ideas have been appropriated from a "commons", or a shared domain of ideas which is not significantly devalued by the removal of that idea. This idea can then be made the property of that individual without breaching the non-waste condition.

One common interpretation of Locke's labour theory of property (and one which is sometimes treated as a separate justification for intellectual property) is the labour-desert or value-added theory. This position holds that when labour produces something of value to others — something beyond what morality requires the labourer to produce as a contributing member of society — then the labourer *deserves* some benefit. It is only morally right to reward them for their labour with property rights in the thing they produced. In many ways, this normative approach to Locke's labour justification coheres with people's common sense understanding of intellectual creation. Many of us would agree that people have the right, or that they deserve, to enjoy the fruits of their labours, intellectual and otherwise. How the fruits of those labours are constituted often becomes a point of contention, however.

There have been a number of critiques that have been levelled at the labour theory of property as it applies to intellectual property. Critics have suggested that, with respect to ideas, it is false to ascribe the intellectual labour to only one individual — every idea, they suggest, is drawing on a deep historical, cultural storehouse of knowledge. Others ask why we need reward this labour with exclusive property rights, and suggest there are other possible rewards. Still others are concerned that some expressions protected as intellectual property, a bank account application form, for example, seem to require very little intellectual labour, whereas a novel requires much effort of the mind and that both of these activities receive the same rights. Finally, some critics complain that the market value of intellectual property often bears little or no relationship with the significance or amount of labour deployed in its production.

The second philosophical justification for property rights in general, and intellectual property rights in particular, is drawn from the work of enlightenment philosopher G.W.F. Hegel, and rests upon his theory of personality. This approach suggests that property provides a unique or especially suitable mechanism for self-actualization, for personal expression and for dignity and recognition as an individual person. For Hegel, property was personality embodied. Forms of creation such as novels, art, poetry and so on, because of their intimate connection to their creator, are understood as reflective and productive of that individual's personality and thus as belonging to them. To hold otherwise would be to allow another to own us, which is not morally acceptable. Our mutual recognition of other individuals as property owners permits us to engage in contractual relations with them. Both subject and object are enriched and given significance through this encounter Hegel claims.

There are criticisms of this rationale as well. First, critics observe that not all intellectual property products appear to have human personality at stake in their creation — for example, databases, compilations or maps. Further, it is unclear under this rationale how one would take account of common, public or shared property. Finally, while the theory may justify how property is created, it provides little guidance as to how that property should circulate in a market economy.

Finally, the third justification offered as to why a society should recognize intellectual property rights in creative expression is an argument of economic efficiency. It draws its philosophical basis from social utilitarian theory. This rationale suggests that we reward intellectual property rights to creators so that they will continue to work. Intellectual property thus stimulates innovation and creativity, and thereby improves society. It assumes that there are insufficient other incentives for creators to put in the necessary time, effort and resources to create. This justification has constitutional force in the United States where intellectual property rights exist "to promote the progress of science and the useful arts".

However, the utilitarian rationale contains within it the paradox that we give exclusive rights to owners of intellectual property, placing what would otherwise be common property into private hands, in order to generate more expressive material in the public domain. Some critics argue that the rationale does not work in practice and that intellectual property stifles, rather than stimulates, creation. Others suggest that creators would express themselves even without the intellectual property incentive. Some note that there are other ways to remunerate creators than with full property rights, while others claim the relationship between the social good and some forms of intellectual property is uncertain, and further that there needs to be more recognition of a hierarchy of social goods.

Until the 1990s, the legitimacy of intellectual property was rarely questioned. However, in the last 20 years this has changed. The legal regimes protecting intellectual property rights were always intended as a balance of the rights given to creators in the short term with the more robust cultural commons for everyone that would result in the long term. Yet, all around us — in disputes between researchers in the North and the communities in the South over biopatents, in the ongoing struggles of file-sharers and the media industries, or in the fights between anti-globalization activists and owners of corporate trademarks — the balance seems to be increasingly unequal. We can see the edges of these justifications fraying as intellectual property issues percolate through the public consciousness and people begin to question what is happening to freedom of expression.

This questioning, this concern over the extent of intellectual property rights and their impacts on the self-expression of ordinary individuals has happened for a number of reasons. As so much of the world's economy has shifted towards a reliance upon information, the economic, political, social and cultural significance of intellectual property has increased dramatically. The value of intellectual property assets in the corporate world has increased exponentially since the 1970s. There has been a corresponding homogenization, strengthening and extension of intellectual property law globally through international legal and economic cooperation. However, at the same time, now that much of our expression can be digitized and moved around the world at an incredible speed and at a very low cost, access to a wealth of expressive material has opened up for a much larger number of people. This global population is increasingly questioning the restrictions on its expression posed by the national and international intellectual property regimes. The very same technologies that are enabling unprecedented access to information and expression are being used by owners to control and defend their property rights. However, as we have seen repeatedly in the various generations of file-sharing software, this control is never complete. Users are also deploying technology to thwart ownership rights. It is against this backdrop of digitization, globalization, propertization, legalization and user mobilization that the recent copyright and trademark battles of Canadians have played out. The stakes are high as we struggle to make sense of how the propertization of various forms of communication limits and shapes how we can express ourselves in Canada and around the world.

III. THE PUSH-PULL OF THE CANADIAN COPYRIGHT ARENA

Copyrights are all around us. We all hold copyrights, we all use copyrighted materials every day, in our work and in our play, and more than ever we are realizing the political stakes of copyright. In Canada, the copyright domain is characterized by two conflicting approaches to how to address the impact of digital technology on copyright as a regulatory mechanism. The approach of the government has generally been in favour of the strengthening of owners' rights in line with the direction taken in the United States with their 1998 legislation, the *Digital Millennium Copyright Act*[3] (DMCA). However, the implementation of this move towards strengthening owners' rights in a digital era has been slow and, as we shall see, there have been some interesting consequences to the delayed pace of actual legislative change. The approach of Canadian courts in a series of landmark decisions over the last decade has been to advocate for the public interest and for users.

A. Copyright Law

Copyright means, literally, the right to copy. And this right is governed exclusively by federal legislation in Canada, the *Copyright Act*.[4] The Department of Industry Canada administers the legislation, although both Industry Canada and the Department of Canadian Heritage are responsible for the development of policy. As in the carriage and content division of communications regulation discussed in Chapter 1, Industry and Heritage have favoured different approaches, anchored in different regulatory logics, and resulting in some tensions and delays in the copyright policy-making process.

Copyright legislation in Canada predates Confederation, but the drafters of the constitution gave to the federal government jurisdiction over copyright in the *Constitution Act, 1867*. From that time until 1921, there was a series of Imperial, provincial and federal laws that applied to copyright. In 1921, the federal government consolidated and made exclusive a new *Copyright Act* which came into force in 1924. The

---

[3] Pub. L. No. 105-304, 112 Stat. 2860 (1998).
[4] R.S.C. 1985, c. C-42.

legislation underwent major amendments in 1931, with the addition of what are known as moral rights for creators. The next significant round of amendments occurred in 1988 when computer programs were brought within the purview of the legislation. Canada signing the North American Free Trade Agreement (NAFTA) and the World Trade Organization (WTO) Agreement on Trade-Related Aspects of Intellectual Property Rights (TRIPS) resulted in further revisions in 1993 and 1994. In 1997, Canada became a signatory to two World Intellectual Property Organization (WIPO) treaties: the WIPO Copyright Treaty (WCT) and the WIPO Performances and Phonograms Treaty (WPPT). Changes were made to the legislation then to recognize "neighbouring rights" in light of the WPPT. Neighbouring rights are the rights of performers, record producers and broadcasters, whose rights to circulate content are protected even though they themselves have not created anything. The 1997 legislative amendments also contained provision for what is known as the private copying exception for sound recordings — a change not required by Canada's international economic commitments. Canada's private exemption for sound recording is a unique system which permits Canadians to make one copy of a sound recording for personal use without breaching copyright. There is dispute between analysts as to whether the private copying exception is "WIPO-compliant". Twice since 1997, federal governments have tabled significant new legislation to amend the *Copyright Act* designed to move Canada into the digital era and enable Canada to finally ratify the two WIPO treaties. Both proposed bills would have resolved the status of file-sharing activities in Canada, for example. However, in both instances, the negative public response to the proposed legislation has been significant, and combined with the instability of minority government rule, has resulted in both bills dying on the order paper.

In general, the *Copyright Act* grants to copyright owners the sole and exclusive right to reproduce, perform or publish a work, defined as an original literary, dramatic, musical and artistic work, sound recordings and performances. The quality and legality of the work are irrelevant. In other words the trashiest tabloids and the most intellectual novels are both awarded the same rights. Works can be in draft or final state, commercial or personal, published or unpublished, or created by amateurs or professionals.

There are three criteria for determining if something is a "work": originality, fixation and the nationality of its creator and the place of its publication. The criterion of originality is not originality in the layperson's sense of the term and it is important to remember that it applies to the expression, not the idea. Originality within copyright law does not mean completely novel or new. The test, until recently, was that the work only had to originate with the author and not be copied. Recently, as will be discussed later in this chapter, the test has shifted from being a mere "sweat of the brow" test of labour to requiring some level of discernment on the part of the author. Expressions that have been found to be original by courts in Canada include: print and electronic books, songs, paintings, tables, compilations, directories, translations, adaptations, dictionaries, as well as new arrangements of works in which the original copyright has expired.

The second requirement for a work is that it must be fixed, namely "... expressed to some extent at least in some material form, capable of identification and having a more or less permanent endurance".[5] So with music, for example, a musical work is the song itself, not its recording. However, the recording may be a way of fixing the song for copyright purposes, rather than writing it down on staff paper. Broadcasts are taped or scripted in order to ensure that they are fixed. Communications which are unfixed would include: a lecture, speech, address or sermon if there are no notes for it and it is not being recorded, a mere image on a computer screen, or an idea only expressed verbally. Finally, the third requirement is one of jurisdiction. All Canadian creators receive copyright protection automatically in Canada and in most other countries in the world. As well, if the place of publication is in Canada or any of its international partners, then rights accrue.

Outside of employment situations where the employer may hold the copyrights and some historically anachronistic rules for photographers, the first copyright in a work is typically held by the author, defined as the person who first expresses the work in a tangible form. She receives two types of rights, economic and moral. Economic rights include the right to reproduce the work; to perform it publicly; to publish it; to adapt, translate or abridge the work; to transmit it to the public by means of telecommunication; or to authorize anyone else to do those things. Economic rights accrue to the owner of the copyright, whether or not that person is the author of the work. Someone infringes these economic rights by doing anything that the owner has the exclusive right to do. The primary remedies available to the owner include an award of damages or an injunction (or court order) to stop the illegal copying, translation, *etc.* The economic rights in a work can be divided and sold, licensed, given away and so on, either in bundles or as separate rights. Therefore an author can license his copyright to publication to a book publisher, license the right to translate and serialize the work to a magazine, and retain the film rights himself to dispose of later. He may allow a local theatre group to do a reading of an excerpt of the text for free and license

---

5   *Canadian Admiral Corp. v. Rediffusion Inc.*, [1954] Ex. C.R. 382, 20 C.P.R. 75 (Ex. Ct.).

a portion to be put up on the writers' union website under a creative commons licence.[6] Economic rights are reciprocally recognized in almost every country around the world. However, one right that is not yet recognized in Canada is that of "making available", namely the right to make content available to the public by means of the Internet. Combined with Canada's private copying exemption, this is why, at the time of writing, the uploading and downloading of copyrighted content from the Internet is not contrary to Canadian law. This has been a sore spot for American politicians and media industry leaders and much pressure has been placed on Canada to change its legislation.

There is another way that Canada distinguishes itself from its neighbours to the South in terms of copyright, and that is in the recognition of moral rights. Moral rights emerge out of the French civil law tradition in order to protect the honour and reputation of the author. In contrast to economic rights, they accrue to only the author and cannot be bought and sold. However, they can be waived by the author. There are three kinds of moral rights: rights of paternity or attribution, rights of integrity and rights of association. Paternity rights give the author the right to have her name appear or to be near the work, to be anonymous, or to use a pseudonym when the work is exposed to the public. Integrity rights protect the work itself against changes or damages that would alter its quality as an artwork. Finally, the owner is not free to associate a work with a cause, product, service or institution without the consent of the author. One of the best known cases of the successful assertion of moral rights involved visual artist, Michael Snow. He created a sculpture of 60 geese that was on display in Toronto's Eaton Centre. As part of the mall's holiday decorations, it placed red ribbons on the neck of each goose. The artist successfully sued the Centre arguing that the integrity of the work was damaged by their "decoration".[7]

Copyright vests immediately in the creation of a work and does not require any additional registration for validity, although a registry exists for reasons of administrative and evidentiary efficiency. The rights last for the life of the author plus 50 years. Here again, Canada distinguishes itself from the United States where in 1998, the United States Congress passed what came to be known as the Sonny Bono Copyright Amendment. Walt Disney Corporation had lobbied aggressively for a retroactive extension of the term of copyright given its pending loss of rights in some valuable early footage of "Steamboat Willie" to the public domain. The amendment changed the term for individually authored works to life

---

6   See online: <http://www.creativecommons.org>.
7   *Snow v. Eaton Centre Ltd.*, [1982] O.J. No. 3645, 70 C.P.R. (2d) 105 (Ont. H.C.J.).

of the author plus 70 years — an extension of 20 years. The amendment was challenged constitutionally, but was upheld.

Much of the expressive material that we encounter in our daily lives — advertisements, television programs, films, music, books, emails, newspaper articles, videos, databases, letters — are subject to copyrights. So, how is it that we do anything with these texts but passively consume them? The *Copyright Act* provides for several circumstances where we are able to use copyrighted material without infringing the owner's rights. One of the most relevant exceptions for university students is "fair dealing", which in the United States is known as "fair use". Fair dealing is a fairly narrow exception but includes use for the purposes of study, research, criticism, review or newspaper summary provided the author is cited. There are also some provisions for parody; the public recitation of extracts; the use of the work in legislative, judicial or administrative proceedings; and use for purposes of repairs and modifications. One can also make a back-up of a computer program, draw or photograph a work in public display, and libraries, archives and newspapers have some additional protections.

Most commonly used by ordinary Canadians is what is known as our private copying exception. This is a rather ingenious system that was developed by the Canadian government and the music industry to address the issue of home recording in the 1980s. When it became apparent that people were going to use cassette tapes to record sound content from the radio and from other cassettes and LP records, rather than fight this, the music industry in Canada proposed the private copying exception. All Canadians pay a small levy on blank sound recording media such as cassettes and recordable CDs when they buy them in the store.[8] This money is collected by the retailer and is provided to an artists' collective, in this case, the Society of Composers, Authors and Publishers of Music in Canada (SOCAN). SOCAN then distributes the funds to artists. While this system has its critics concerned about the time delays and fairness in the distribution of funds, this is a uniquely Canadian system that recognizes that people will copy music, and finds an alternative way to deal with it than prosecuting them. The United States does not approve of Canada's private copying exemption because, in principle, it suggests, the provision makes legal what would otherwise be illegal, copying. It is a point that has come up repeatedly in negotiations between the two countries; however, interestingly, in both sets of recent proposed legislative changes in Canada, the private copying exception has survived unscathed.

---

[8] The levy for CDs in 2009, for example, was 29 cents.

B. The Policy Reform Process

The Canadian government has been involved in a protracted, multi-year copyright reform process with national and international dimensions. The major catalyst to this round of amendments was the signing of the two WIPO treaties, as noted above. There are a number of provisions under the WIPO treaties that are in dispute in Canada. These include: the making available right (to address the uploading of files through file-sharing software); digital rights management (the various technologies which enable owners to control or eliminate digital copying regardless of context); criminalizing the cracking of copy-protection programs or technology; the status of Canada's private copying exception; and an overall ethic of international harmonization in the direction of the American *DMCA*.

In 2001, the Canadian government launched its latest policy process with its document, *A Framework for Copyright Reform*. It also issued two consultation papers — one on Internet retransmission issues and the other a broader analysis of digital copyright issues. The call for submissions received a relatively large number of responses for such a hearing, indicating not only significant interest in the issue on the part of the public, but also the beginnings of a more organized grassroots movement in Canada, supported by similar organizations within the United States, to lobby government and engage public opinion. The retransmission issues were addressed by Bill C-11 which came into force in 2003. This basically provided Internet Service Providers with protection when merely retransmitting content. Their provision of service is not a "communication to the public" for the purposes of the legislation. This was in keeping with the CRTC's approach of letting ISPs do what they do given they are the technological backbone of the Internet, provided that they do nothing to the content.

The digital copyright issues were much more contentious, and further consultations were held in 2002. Late that year, the government tabled to Parliament a report called: *Supporting Culture and Innovation: Report on the Provisions and Operations of the Copyright Act*. The document was the outcome of the five-year review required by the legislation as a result of the 1997 revisions and is known as the "Section 92 Report". The Section 92 Report reiterated the Canadian government's commitment to bringing our legislation into conformity with the WIPO treaties, provided that the issues were analyzed and appropriate consultations took place. It identified a series of short-, medium- and long-term goals to be addressed through the reform process, ranging from liability for ISPs to Aboriginal knowledge in the digital age. Further to the section 92 review, the Standing Committee on Canadian Heritage began its review and adopted a resolution recommending that the Ministers of Canadian Heritage and

Industry prepare legislation to implement the treaties in 2004. This did not take place and the committee began hearings on the short-term issues such as: private copying and WIPO ratification, photographic works, ISP liability, use of Internet material for educational purposes, learning enhanced technology and interlibrary loans.

Its report, entitled *Interim Report on Copyright Reform* made nine recommendations in May of 2004. These included that the government ratify the treaties immediately, that photographers receive the same authorship rights as other creators, that ISPs be made potentially liable for copyrighted material circulated on their facilities, that a licensing regime be implemented to charge fees for Internet material used for educational purposes, that inter-library loan material also be subjected to licensing, and that the government move on these issues very quickly. This report was widely and stridently criticized, particularly with respect to its stance on licensing materials to educational institutions already in the public domain. Critics charged that the Committee acted in haste, its consultations focused on industry and that Canada was merely adopting an approach similar to the Draconian *DMCA* of the United States.

A federal election meant that the recommendations were not acted upon until the summer of 2005 when first reading was given to Bill C-60 — the first of the Canadian government's abortive attempts to revise the *Copyright Act*. The legislation died with the fall of the liberal government in December of that year, however, not before it received significant criticism for its move in the general direction of an enhanced regime for owners.

What had been taking place since 2001, however, was the politicization of the Canadian public on issues of copyright. Numerous interest groups formed devoted to scrutinizing government action on copyright issues. A critical mass of Canadians shifted from being passive consumers to active users, which complicated the government's approach. In late 2007, the Conservative government leaked that it was going to be bringing in amendments to the *Copyright Act*, and within three days, more than 40,000 Canadians had joined a fair copyright Facebook group demanding changes. The numbers continued to rise in subsequent weeks. Canadians wrote their Members of Parliament, emailed the Prime Minister and signed petitions. As a result, the government held off on the bill and the subsequent version contained changes that were clearly calculated to address consumer concerns.

In June 2008 the government introduced Bill C-61 proposing substantial amendments to the *Copyright Act*. It, too, died on the order paper when the government took its break for the summer, but it is likely that a revised version will reappear in late 2010. Some of the most significant provisions in the proposed legislation included retaining the protections for Internet Service Providers, yet at the same time requiring them to maintain documentation that would permit the identification of users. Criminal penalties were put in place for anyone who circumvents the technological protection measures that owners place on their media to prevent copying (and no provision was made to make exceptions for fair dealing). Consumers were permitted to legally record television programs for later viewing — time shifting — but the time periods for which one could retain the recording were short and were limited to VHS and not DVD, PVRs, *etc.* Consumers could device shift — transfer legally recorded music onto other devices — only if they did not circumvent copy protections, but the rules were complicated and the digital locks placed by owners on their media made this provision increasingly moot. Protections with respect to photographs, which had long been an historical anachronism, were changed so that they would be dealt with in the same manner as other works. The much-contested "making available right" was included allowing performers and sound recorders the right to control the posting of their work on the Internet. In a gesture towards file-sharing citizens, the legislation limited the amount of damages that could be awarded against someone for downloading music for private use to $500. Rather than re-propose the same legislation, the government has committed to further consultations, suggesting perhaps that it recognizes the emergent Canadian copyright consciousness. The most recent round of consultations concluded in fall 2009, with the government receiving an overwhelming amount of submissions compared to other public consultations.

Canada, as mentioned above, makes a very interesting case study in copyright reform. First, because our reform process has been much slower than that of the United States, permitting greater reflection and public contestation. However, the second reason is that copyright owners have recently lost a series of important cases in Canada where the courts have been very clear that they are going to include in any examination of copyright a consideration of the public interest. They are concerned to ensure users' rights are not trampled in the rush to protect owners' rights in digital content.

C. The Copyright Cases

While the public interest and need to protect the balance of rights at the heart of intellectual property are present as rhetorics in the policy reform process, they have been progressively muted in favour of bringing Canada in line with its global trading partners. Interestingly, and surprising to some, where the public interest has received its most rousing support has been in Canada's courts. We will take up three landmark decisions that give legal endorsement to the overall ethos that users' rights, the public interest and the balance in copyright is something the courts are embracing.

A case involving the lowly technology of the photocopier broke new ground in Canadian copyright law in 2004 and went a significant way towards restoring the balance inherent in the intellectual property bargain. The Law Society of Upper Canada, which maintains and operates the Law Library at the University of Toronto, was sued by CCH Canadian Limited, a publisher of legal materials. CCH argued that three practices by the Library constituted breach of its copyrights: first, the library provided a custom photocopy service to in-library researchers; second, it offered a photocopy machine on the premises for clients to make their own photocopies; and third, it offered a fax service to send materials to clients who could not come to the library.

The high court began by reiterating its position on balance in copyright:

> The *Copyright Act* is usually presented as a balance between promoting the public interest in the encouragement and dissemination of works of the arts and intellect and obtaining a just reward for the creator ... The proper balance among these and other public policy objectives lies not only in recognizing the creator's rights *but in giving due weight to their limited nature*. In interpreting the *Copyright Act*, courts should strive to maintain an appropriate balance between these two goals.[9]

The court then rewrote the originality standard, suggesting that if too low a standard is used, that tips the balance in favour of creators. While a work does not have to be novel or unique, it must not be copied and it must be the outcome of the exercise of skill and judgement (which could not be characterized as a purely mechanical exercise). Skill involves the use of knowledge, developed aptitude or practiced ability whereas judgement involves "one's capacity for discernment or ability to form an opinion or evaluation by comparing different possible options in producing the work".[10]

On the issue of the self-service photocopiers, the court had to define what constituted authorization and confirmed that merely providing the means to copy something is not considered authorization. The library was entitled to assume its patrons were using the photocopy machines legally and that it was not required to control, or take responsibility for, its patrons. A third key issue the court addressed was that of fair dealing.

---

[9] *CCH Canadian Ltd. v. Law Society of Upper Canada*, [2004] S.C.J. No. 12, [2004] 1 S.C.R. 339 at para. 10 (S.C.C.). [Emphasis added].

[10] *Ibid.*, at para. 26.

In the past, the fair dealing exception had been quite narrow. The court in *CCH* not only expanded it, but went further to redefine fair dealing as a "user's right", rather than as a mere defence to copyright infringement.

> [T]he fair dealing exception is perhaps more properly understood as an integral part of the *Copyright Act* than simply a defence. Any act falling within the fair dealing exception will not be an infringement of copyright. The fair dealing exception, like other exceptions in the *Copyright Act*, is a user's right. In order to maintain the proper balance between the rights of a copyright owner and users' interests, it must not be interpreted restrictively. As Professor Vaver, *supra*, has explained, at p. 171: "User rights are not just loopholes. Both owner rights and user rights should therefore be given the fair and balanced reading that befits remedial legislation."[11]

The characterization of the exception in a language of users' rights is a very significant endorsement of the individual's right to free expression in relation to copyrighted material.

Thus, the publisher lost on all grounds and those who used the copyrighted materials won. Even more significantly, Canada's highest court unanimously endorsed the idea, not merely of public interest within the legislation, but also of express rights on the part of individual users. And although the case involved photocopy machines, it would soon have a much greater impact in a different technological arena.

In 2004, the Canadian Recording Industry Association (CRIA), following the lead of its American counterpart, brought legal action for copyright infringement against 29 unknown individual Internet users who allegedly had swapped more than 1,000 digital music files each using peer-to-peer file-sharing programs such as KaZaA and iMesh. The Copyright Board, which makes policy on copyright issues, had previously held that because of the private copying exception and the resulting levy paid on blank recording media, downloading music for personal use was not illegal in Canada. To avoid this, the CRIA brought its suit specifically against individuals that were said to be *uploading* files to the Internet; however, it could not identify the individual defendants. The individuals operated under pseudonyms. Because it had their Internet Protocol addresses, the CRIA brought an action to force the ISPs to reveal the identities of the account holders associated with those IP addresses. Thus, the privacy rights of the individual clients of the ISPs were pitted against the copyrights held by artists and the recording industry. One of the ISPs refused to allow its clients to be identified and the case went to court.

---

[11]   *Ibid.*, at para. 48.

The Federal Court trial judge found that the ISPs could not be required to provide the identities of their clients, and therefore, the action for copyright infringement was stalled in its tracks by the privacy rights of those labelled as "pirates" by the music industry. The judge went further, however, commenting that the uploading of music was not a breach of copyright. The decision turned on more technical grounds concerning the affidavit evidence provided and so all comments with respect to the infringement of copyright are considered extraneous to the binding aspects of the decision. However, this was the first Canadian judicial pronouncement on the issue of peer-to-peer file-sharing and so was being watched by industry actors, pundits and file-sharers in Canada and around the world.

The judge confirmed that downloading a song for personal use is not an infringement in Canada because of the private copying exception. CRIA argued that downloading and uploading music files constituted reproduction, authorization, distribution or possession for the purpose of distribution. The judge felt that the nature of the software involved merely placing copies of the files on shared directories available to other users, and that this activity did not constitute distribution or authorization. The judge drew a parallel between file-sharing and the photocopier in the library:

> ... setting up facilities that allow copying does not amount to author-izing infringement. I cannot see a real difference between a library that places a photocopy machine in a room full of copyrighted material and a computer user that places a personal copy on a shared directory linked to a P2P service. In either case the preconditions to copying and infringement are set up but the element of authorization is missing.[12]

Finally, the judge held that merely placing a copy on a shared directory was not distribution either because there was no positive act such as sending out copies or advertising.

This decision flew in the face of international practice and received a lot of global media attention. The CRIA appealed to the Federal Court of Appeal. In 2005, the Appeal Court overturned the decision on the eviden-tiary point, but went on to say that the judge should not have commented on the substance of the file-sharing issue, that everything he said was *obiter dicta* (extraneous to the proper legal resolution of the matter), and possibly prejudicial to the case. Ultimately CRIA dropped the case because the evidence it had was too poor and to date no other file-sharing case has been prosecuted to that level.

---

[12] *BMG Canada Inc. v. John Doe*, [2004] F.C.J. No. 525, 2004 FC 488 at para. 27 (F.C.T.D.).

Finally, in 2004, the Supreme Court of Canada at last resolved a nine-year-old dispute that had come to be known as the Tariff 22 case. SOCAN, Canada's leading music collective, was seeking a way to make money from downloaded music. Further to the 1989 amendments that gave to owners the right to communicate by telecommunication, they wanted ISPs to be required to collect royalties for downloaded music, the way retailers collect fees on blank audio recording media. The Canadian Association of Internet Providers were resisting this because they wanted to maintain the neutral status that they have in both the communications legal framework as well as in the *Copyright Act*.

SOCAN first applied to the Copyright Board for the tariff in 1995 and after four years of hearings, the Board found that the ISPs did not have to collect the tariff. SOCAN appealed to the Federal Court of Canada and that court held in 2002 that ISPs might be required to pay some royalties on the grounds of their practices of caching content. However, this was overturned by the Supreme Court of Canada in another strong statement for copyright balance in the digital age.

The Court recognized the challenge of applying legislation designed 100 years ago to technologies its drafters could not have imagined. However, in the absence of the ratification of the WIPO treaties, the Court signalled it would not read into the current law provisions only proposed in the reform process. Again, the Court asserted the need for balance in the interpretation of the *Copyright Act*, this time explicitly in relation to the Internet.

> The capacity of the Internet to disseminate "works of the arts and intellect" is one of the great innovations of the information age. Its use should be facilitated rather than discouraged, but this should not be done unfairly at the expense of those who created the works of arts and intellect in the first place.[13]

The entire Court clearly endorsed the protection offered to ISPs, recognizing that the legislation clearly defines ISPs as service, and not content, providers. This is not merely an immunity from infringement, but rather, they are not infringing the right in the first place. As long as the ISP does not meddle in the content, it is not communicating the work to the public for the purposes of copyright, even if that content violates copyrights. However, the case required closer examination of how the Internet works. SOCAN argued that in caching some of the content — namely making a temporary copy on the ISP server so that the data can be transmitted more quickly — the ISPs had acted as more than mere

---

[13]   *Society of Composers, Authors and Music Publishers of Canada v. Canadian Association of Internet Providers*, [2004] S.C.J. No. 44, [2004] 2 S.C.R. 427 at para. 40 (S.C.C.).

conduits. The Court held, consistently with the position taken by the CRTC and the government of Canada previously, that liability for caching would chill the expansion and development of the Internet. It held that a cache copy was part of doing regular business, was content-neutral, and that ISPs could use caching technology to improve service to their clients without concern as to liability.

The issue of authorization came up in this case as well as SOCAN argued that the ISPs knew very well that people were using their facilities for file-sharing. The Court, following its own more stringent definition of authorization from *CCH*, held that knowing that someone might be using the technology to violate copyright is not enough. If an ISP were notified of the offending content and refused to deal with the issue, this might constitute authorization.

Thus, in this interesting set of copyright cases, the courts have radically altered the Canadian copyright terrain, much more quickly and effectively than the reform process has. The need to seek a balance between owners' interests and the public interest has been reinstated. The bar has been raised on the test for originality so that there is some discernment and limits in what attracts copyright. Authorization has been confirmed as something which should be strictly interpreted. Further, providing the technology for reproduction, alone, is not sufficient to garner liability, nor is suspecting that someone might be doing something illegal. ISPs are fully protected from liability provided they act as conduits only and technical arguments such as that made around caching will not be seen to undermine the policy directive from Parliament. Most importantly, the courts have begun to speak of users as a recognized group, as a group with rights — both to access copyrighted material and to the respect of their privacy. The *Copyright Act* has been framed as a piece of legislation that can and should protect the rights of users as well as owners. Therefore, through its courts, Canada is going against the global consensus to ensure that the copyright regime does not unduly restrain freedom of expression. This is not dissimilar to the efforts being made by Canadian courts in the area of trademarks as well, as we shall see.

IV. LIMITING THE PROPERTIZATION OF EXPRESSION: TRADEMARKS IN CANADA

A trademark is a way of marking a producer's good or service to distinguish its source from that of another producer's products. The trademark regime takes as its goals the protection of, and assistance to, the consumer, as well as encouraging fairness between competitors in the marketplace.

This practice of marking goods is protected in Canada at common law and under federal legislation, the *Trade-marks Act*.[14] What makes trademarks particularly relevant for an assessment of freedom of expression however, is that they have emerged as the favoured legal vehicle for what David Bollier (2005) has called "brand-name bullying", namely the intimidation of ordinary citizens by intellectual property rights owners regardless of the defensibility of their legal position.[15] Increasingly, trademark owners are policing their marks, not just in their particular area of business, but more broadly as private property cultural symbols in their own right. For example, McDonald's threatened legal action against a small restaurant calling itself "McSushi"; Walt Disney pursued a children's daycare which had painted some of its animated characters on its wall; and MGM Studios went after a gay-rights group for their street safety initiative called "the Pink Panther Patrol". It is these sorts of practices where the expression of ordinary citizens — sometimes commercial, sometimes critical, sometimes parodic, sometimes incidental — is intersecting with the trademark claims (not always legitimate) of large corporate owners that raise issues of freedom of expression.

The registration of trademarks in Canada dates back to Confederation and the current form of our legislation to revisions made in the early 1950s. Unlike copyright law, the *Trade-marks Act* does not replace common law rights, but exists as an alternative regime. Interestingly, trademarks, unlike copyright and most other forms of intellectual property, are not about the protection or support of intellectual activity. The law does not read a trade-mark as a creative expression and does not grant rights for the labour or creativity that may go into its production. Property rights in a trademark arise from its use in a marketplace and the rights are held, not by the creator, but by the user. Canada is distinguishing itself in the global arena in the domain of trademarks as well, by taking its own path. There has been a lot of legal activity in recent years, and to date, the Supreme Court of Canada has refused to allow the domination of large corporate brands to the extent that the United States has witnessed. There remains an attentiveness to not only the consumer's interest, but also to the public interest in a robust cultural commons that has not been fully enclosed, or rendered into private property.[16] Here we will focus on the statutory law and its interpretation by the Supreme Court.

---

[14] R.S.C. 1985, c. T-13.
[15] Bollier, David. *Brand Name Bullies: The Quest to Own and Control Culture* (New York: Wiley, 2005).
[16] For an interesting discussion of the enclosure of the cultural commons, see James Boyle. *The Public Domain: Enclosing the Commons of the Mind* (New Haven, CT: Yale University Press, 2008).

A. Trademark Law

A trademark is defined in the legislation as a mark that distinguishes the products or services of one trader from those of another, specifically by indicating the source or origin of the trader's goods or services. There are three necessary elements to a trademark: the expression in question must be a "mark", it must be distinctive or capable of becoming distinctive, and it must be "used" as a trademark. A mark encompasses "any sign, or any combination of signs ... including personal names, designs, letters, numerals, colors, figurative elements."[17] It must be visible and distinct from the product itself. Theoretically, virtually any expression that could be used to distinguish goods or services can be a legitimate trademark and as the creativity of the marketing industry expands, so does the range of legal trademarks. Examples include a word, such as IBM, Zeller's, or Xerox; a phrase or slogan, such as "Mr. Christie You Make Good Cookies" or "If Life Were Like This, You Wouldn't Need a Visa Card"; a logo or design, the famous McDonald's "M" or the apple on Mac computers; or even a distinctive shape such as the Coke bottle, the Toblerone chocolate bar, or the Absolut vodka bottle. There are also a number of protected official trademarks that certify standards, designate government institutions, and so on.

A trademark must either actually distinguish the products or services between firms or be adapted to distinguish them. Words, phrases or images that are created specifically for a particular product, are highly distinctive. For example, KODAK refers only to the camera company because it was invented for that purpose and is not a word, otherwise, in English. "Scotties Little Softies" however, by using common words, must gain its distinction in use in relation to bathroom tissue. In the ebb and flow of business, trademarks gain and lose their distinctiveness. If a trademark is challenged, its owner must be able to demonstrate that it is distinctive or the mark loses its validity. In short, a non-distinctive trademark is not. The reason for the loss of distinctiveness is irrelevant; the test is whether or not the public might be confused. Distinctiveness can be lost by a product being too successful, namely, the mark has become the generic name for that type of product. Some famous examples include: gramophone, nylon, band-aid, shredded wheat and hoover. Distinction is also lost if the mark is used by more than one business at a time; thus, companies need to police the use of their marks (or similar marks) by others.

The third requirement for a trademark is that it be used. For services, a mark is used if it is displayed in performing or advertising the service.

---

[17] Contained in the TRIPS agreement.

For goods, it has to appear on the goods themselves, on the packaging, or the consumer has to be notified at the point of purchase. The first to use a mark is generally the one entitled to its registration. The use requirement is one that recognizes that trademarks are about communication in an active marketplace. If a business is not using its mark, this rationale suggests that someone else should be able to do so.

Certain communications cannot be trademarked. One cannot trademark the name of another person (living or dead within the last 30 years) if it is not the name of the person seeking the trademark. Marks cannot be descriptive or misdescriptive of the goods with which they are associated. For example, one could not trademark "Homemade Bread" for a line of homemade artisinal bread products because it would be descriptive. The justification for this is that it would place unfair limits on the rights of other similar businesses to trademark the basic descriptors of their product or business. On the other hand, the makers of the "Shammi" — a transparent polyethylene glove for washing cars and windows — was not a proper trademark because the glove did not have any traces of chamois in it. The name might have misled consumers into thinking that they were purchasing a real chamois product. A trademark cannot be the name of the goods or services in any language and so SCHERE was not a registrable mark for scissors as it is the German word for scissors. Offensive marks — those that are scandalous, obscene or immoral — cannot be used, although this has not been a significant issue in Canada. Marks cannot falsely suggest a connection with a living or recently deceased individual; therefore, I could not trademark "Shatner's Flakes" for bran cereal given the implied connection to actor William Shatner. And of course, the mark cannot be confusing with an existing trademark — the *raison d'être* of the trademark regime. Analysts suggest that, at present, the bar is pretty low in Canada in terms of what cannot be trademarked and vendors are becoming increasingly savvy in how they are constructing their trademarks.

In order to receive trademark protection, the mark's user must file an application to register it; the mark is then evaluated against the requirements of the legislation and examined in comparison with existing marks for those types of goods or services and if it clears those requirements, is registered. All trademarks must be registered in relation to the type of good or service with which they will be associated and in fact, the trademark is only a trademark for that particular type of good or service. If someone has registered the trademark "Harvey's" for the provisions of fast food, then that would not preclude another person from registering the trademark of "Harvey's" in relation to the sale of sporting goods. The assumption is that these businesses are competing in very different markets and there is little to no risk of confusion to the consuming public. This is an element of trademark law that is seemingly forgotten when large corporations with substantial investments in their brands begin to claim their marks in all markets.

In Canada, a registered trademark lasts for a period of 15 years, renewable indefinitely provided the mark remains distinctive. Registration provides the owner with four primary rights, the breach of which provoke remedies similar to copyright infringement. First, the registered owner has the exclusive right to use the trademark. Thus, the vendors selling counterfeit Rolex watches or Louis Vuitton handbags are violating the trademarks of the Rolex and Louis Vuitton companies. Second, the owner has the right to be free of the use of a confusingly similar trademark by someone else. The test for confusion is whether the ordinary customer or unwary purchaser would believe the product or service of one vendor is likely to be related to the product or service of another. The Federal Court of Appeal held, for example, that a beauty products business called "Pink Panther Beauty Corporation" did not infringe the trademark of United Artists Corporation in relation to the series of films starring Peter Sellers, and more recently Steve Martin. While the Court recognized that famous trademarks have a greater mobility across businesses than others — a greater recognition value — the Court found it extremely unlikely that anyone would be confused that the movie company was the source of the beauty products. Third, the owner is protected from someone else using his trademark in a way that will dilute it, or depreciate the goodwill attached to the mark. In 1996, the Michelin tire company was able to argue that the use by the Canadian Auto Workers union of its iconic trademarked image, the Michelin Man, depreciated its goodwill. The union had produced a leaflet with an image of the Michelin Man stomping upon a worker during a campaign to unionize. The union argued its use was parody and constituted free expression. In a much-criticized decision, the Federal Court held that freedom of expression could not serve as a defence to a copyright or trademark violation. The Court held further that parody or criticism as exceptions to intellectual property rights should be narrowly interpreted. As we shall see, however, this issue is once again before the courts. Fourth and finally, as with copyright, the owner also receives the right to authorize anyone to exercise any of her rights.

The United States has much stronger dilution laws than Canada, particularly after it passed the *Trademark Dilution Revision Act of 2006*.[18] This legislation permits owners of "famous marks", such as Starbucks or

---

[18] Pub. L. No. 109-312 120 Stat. 1730. The legislation was originally passed in 1995 but it required the demonstration of actual economic damage. The most recent amendment has removed that requirement.

Coca-Cola, for example, to defend against potentially confusing marks in any market of goods or services, without the need to demonstrate any actual economic damage from the use of a similar mark. Not all recognizable marks will meet the test of a famous mark; however, once they do, the resulting rights are significant. Owners of famous marks can argue that the purveyor of Starbucks baby clothes weakens the connection in the mind of the consumer between the coffee purveyor's mark and its goods and services. Or, if a cigarette company wanted to register the trademark "Evian", the bottled water seller could object that this might tarnish their mark by its association with something unsavoury or unwholesome, thereby harming the reputation of the mark and its owner. There are fair use exceptions built into the legislation that would protect critics, parodists and non-commercial users. However, what often happens is that a parodist, critic or fan receives a "cease and desist" letter in the mail from the lawyer of the major corporation which owns the allegedly famous mark. While the corporation's lawyers may well suspect that the use would fall within the fair use exceptions in the *Lanham Act*,[19] the recipient of the letter often ceases to use the trademark because he or she does not have the resources to fight the issue in the legal system. While no similar reforms have taken place in Canadian trademark law, these issues have received recent consideration by Canada's courts which are, once again, taking their own path.

B. The Trademark Cases

Not unlike the domain of copyright law in Canada, it is the courts which, in recent years, have been the defenders of freedom of expression in Canadian trademark law, signalling that in the absence of legislation similar to that for dilution in the United States, they will scrutinize each case on its merits and apply the test of the likelihood of confusion to the consumer in determining if the use of a mark should be prohibited. Three recent Supreme Court of Canada decisions have established an interpretive, principled context in which, absent legislative change, future Canadian trademark and expression battles will play out.

In the first case, toy manufacturer, Kirkbi, held the patents for the well-known LEGO construction sets.[20] When its patent expired, Ritvik Holdings, now known as Mega Bloks, started to manufacture and sell plastic bricks interchangeable with LEGO. Kirkbi tried to assert an unregistered trademark in the "LEGO-indicia", namely the upper surface of the block with the raised bumps distributed in an even geometric

---

[19] 15 U.S.C.
[20] *Kirkbi A.G. v. Ritvik Holdings Inc.*, [2005] S.C.J. No. 66, [2005] 3 S.C.R. 302 (S.C.C.).

pattern. The trial judge held that the purely functional features of the LEGO indicia could not become the basis of a trademark, registered or unregistered.

The issue in the Supreme Court of Canada became the constitutionality of the section in the *Trade-marks Act* recognizing unregistered trademarks. The constitutional argument is not particularly pertinent for us; suffice it to say that the Supreme Court upheld Parliament's power to incorporate the common law regime for trademarks. When it turned to considering patents and trademarks, however, the Court began by recognizing:

> The vast and expanding domain of the law of intellectual property is going through a period of major and rapid changes. The pressures of globalization and technological change challenge its institutions, its classifications and sometimes settled doctrines. ... The economic value of intellectual property rights arouses the imagination and litigiousness of rights holders in their search for continuing protection of what they view as their rightful property. Such a search carries with it the risk of discarding basic and necessary distinctions between different forms of intellectual property and their legal and economic functions.[21]

The Court held that the trademark had been properly rejected because its primary purpose was functional, not aesthetic, and therefore it did not qualify as a trademark. Here, Kirkbi was claiming an unregistered trademark consisting solely of the technical or functional characteristics of the LEGO bricks. The Court held that a purely functional design cannot be the basis of a trademark and trademark law should not be used to perpetuate monopoly rights enjoyed under now-expired patents. Most importantly, the Court, while recognizing the reliance of current markets on the power of brands and their incredible economic value, cautioned that we must not confuse the mark with the product itself.

The next two trademark law cases out of the Supreme Court of Canada took on the issue of famous marks and their status in Canadian law. The first case involved a Montreal barbeque restaurant called "Barbie's" which ran afoul of Mattel corporation when it applied for a trademark for its name.[22] In the administrative proceeding it had been found that Barbie's fame was connected to dolls and doll accessories and that the application by the numbered company was for very different products and services, not likely at all to be confusing with the Barbie marks owned by Mattel.

---

[21] *Ibid.*, at para. 37.

[22] *Mattel Inc. v. 3894207 Canada Inc.*, [2006] S.C.J. No. 23, [2006] 1 S.C.R. 772 (S.C.C.).

The Court recognized that within limits, Barbie has become an iconic figure of popular culture. Its annual sales exceed $1.4 billion around the world. It further held that "[t]he power of attraction of trade-marks and other 'famous brand names' is now recognized as among the most valuable of business assets."[23] It went on, however, suggesting that "whatever their commercial evolution, the legal purpose of trade-marks continues ... to be their use by the owner 'to distinguish wares or services' ...".[24] The court reaffirmed that trademark law was consumer law, used by consumers as a shortcut to obtain what they want in a market economy. The Court updated the test for confusion recognizing that in the current market the law does not require that the consumer be diligent, but nor does it assume that they are a "moron in a hurry". Rather, the Canadian consumer was understood as the "ordinary hurried purchaser" — in other words consumers are increasingly informed, but they are busy and the marketplace is full of products and appeals.

Mattel argued that confusion was irrelevant as the Barbie trademark had transcended the products which it originally served to distinguish. The Court did not dispute this, but suggested that in Canada trademark law could not be used to prevent other parties from using a common name such as Barbie in relation to services that are remote from those that generated the fame of the shapely Mattel doll. On the evidence the Court found that it was not likely that prospective customers would associate whoever owned the doll mark with the restaurant. While the Court conceded that the Barbie trademark might some day exceed its association with dolls and doll accessories, at the present time, it had not done so. In fact, the Court held that even if the restaurant was intending to capitalize on Mattel's Barbie, if the marks were not confusing, then the registration remained valid. The Court was careful to say that "[c]are must be taken not to create a zone of exclusivity and protection that overshoots the purpose of trade-mark law."[25]

The Barbie decision was released as part of a pair of famous trademark cases before the Court, the other involving Veuve Clicquot Ponsardin, the maker of fine champagne, and Boutiques Cliquot, a Quebec-based mid-priced women's clothing line.[26] Veuve Clicquot's trademark appears on its wine of course, but the company has also extended it to a line of high-end fashion wares for men and women. The Supreme Court recognized its famous status: "Veuve Clicquot is undoubtedly famous

---

[23] *Ibid.*, at para. 2.
[24] *Ibid.*
[25] *Ibid.*, at para. 22.
[26] *Veuve Clicquot Ponsardin v. Boutiques Cliquot Ltée*, [2006] S.C.J. No. 22, [2006] 1 S.C.R. 824 (S.C.C.).

and its trade-mark deserves wide protection not only from free-riders but from those who, without any intention of free-riding, nevertheless use in their own business distinguishing marks that create confusion or depreciate the value of the goodwill attaching to [it]."[27] Boutiques Cliquot owned the trademarks Cliquot and "Cliquot Un monde a part". Veuve Clicquot claimed that consumers were likely to be confused into thinking that the women's clothing originated from the French winemaker and that Boutiques Cliquot's use was a dilution of its elite mark.

All levels of court found that there was a very low likelihood of confusion between the luxury company Veuve Clicquot and the Quebec mid-priced women's clothing stores. In short, the Court implied that the goods move in different "circles". On the issue of dilution, the Court held that Veuve Clicquot had to establish that its mark was used, that it was sufficiently well known to have significant goodwill attached to it, that the mark was used by the defendant in a manner that would likely have an effect on that goodwill, and that the likely effect would be to depreciate the value of that goodwill. Goodwill, the Court held, referred to the "positive association that attracts customers toward its owner's wares or services rather than those of its competitors".[28] Relevant factors to be considered in a dilution claim included: the degree of recognition of the mark within the relevant universe of consumers; the volume of sales and market penetration of products associated with the claimant's mark; the extent and duration of advertising and publicity accorded the claimant's mark; the geographic reach of the mark; its degree of inherent or acquired distinctiveness; whether products associated with the mark are confined to a narrow or specialized channel of trade or move in multiple channels; and the extent to which the mark is identified with a particular quality. In other words, it set the bar quite high and Veuve Clicquot's case did not meet it.

This trio of cases revisits trademark law in the current global economic context. Overall, these cases signal that Canadian courts feel that general trademark principles remain sound and can work in our current brand society. Further, while recognizing the incredible value of trademarks and the need to protect famous trademark owners, the court is going to view each case on its circumstances and still look to the fundamental purpose of trademark law — to protect the consumer. Canada's high court has signalled it will not let the owners of famous trademarks colonize the cultural commons at the expense of our freedom of expression. So the brand-name bullies that are raising so much concern in the United

27   *Ibid.*, at para. 2.
28   *Ibid.*, at para. 50.

States with their colonization of expression have not fared as well in Canada.

V. CONCLUSION

A case looming on the Canadian legal horizon promises to have great significance for the intersection of freedom of expression and intellectual property law in general, and trademark law in particular. In 2007, a group of pro-Palestinian activists prepared a four-page mock newspaper based on the *Vancouver Sun* in order to critique what they assert is CanWest's and the *Sun*'s pro-Israeli bias. They "borrowed" the logo, but the spoof paper was very easily distinguished from the original. CanWest sued for infringement of its trademark and the activists are claiming that this is parody and that their freedom of expression is at stake. The case, if it proceeds to the Supreme Court, opens up the possibility for the Court to revisit the *Michelin* case and will once again put the issue of the conflict of freedom of expression with propertized expression directly on the table.

In the interim, Canada is benefiting from its somewhat ambivalent response to the global copyright agenda and the user-friendly reasoning of the Supreme Court of Canada. This has opened the door to a much richer discussion of the rights of individual Canadians and their freedom of expression than has been the case elsewhere in the world. It raises the possibility that we might begin to envision copyright, and intellectual property more broadly, as contributing to, rather than in competition with, freedom of expression. As Carys J. Craig passionately argues about copyright:

> The self is always situated in a cultural world and within a network of social relations. Language and literature, music and art, dance and theatre, films and television programs are all aspects of the cultural world in which we exist. The principle of freedom of expression, analyzed in light of our society's cultural values, is an affirmation of the value that we attach to social interaction and communication between members of our society and of our recognition that this expressive activity is, in turn, fundamental to our own development and self-fulfilment. The copyright system should be regarded as one means by which we seek to ensure this process of cultural exchange.[29]

---

[29] Craig, Carys J. "Putting the Community in Communication: Dissolving the Conflict Between Freedom of Expression and Copyright" (2006) 56 U.T.L.J. 75 at 108.

He feels that rather than being at odds with freedom of expression, we need to rethink copyright as a part of the policy to ensure a vibrant environment of shared and individual communication. In the upcoming legislation, as a result of the unique push-pull of the copyright domain in Canada, hopefully the government will adopt more of a "made-in-Canada" compromise that avoids some of the more problematic elements in the American approach.

This uniquely Canadian approach to balancing the interests of the public with those of the owners of certain instances of expression is also visible in the domain of trademarks. Owners are not being permitted to run roughshod over users' or less powerful owners' rights. At the same time, there still exists a domain of legal protection for propertized expression. The CanWest case will be a particularly interesting opportunity to explore the intimate interaction of intellectual property law and freedom of expression. Does freedom of expression provide a viable defence against a claim of trademark infringement? Canadians await this trial as well as the next incarnation of the *Copyright Act* to see what hangs in the balance.

Chapter 4

Criminalizing Expression: Obscenity and Hate Speech

I. INTRODUCTION

In late 2002, David Ahenakew, former Chief of the Assembly of First Nations, gave a profanity-laced speech at a Federation of Saskatchewan Indian Nations (FSIN) health event in which he discussed, among other things, racism against First Nations peoples in the health care system. In a later interview with a reporter for the *Saskatoon Star-Phoenix*, he launched into a tirade that ended with him blaming World War II on the Jews. He claimed that Hitler did the "right thing" when he "fried" six million Jews to cleanse the world of "disease". He was reviled from all sides and was eventually charged by the Saskatchewan government with "hate speech" under the *Criminal Code*.[1] He was stripped of his Order of Canada and resigned his position in the Senate of the FSIN. Because of the instant and virulent condemnation of his comments, several commentators argued that laws against hate speech are misguided. Their position is that such laws drive these views underground rather than exposing them to the light of day and universal condemnation as rightfully, they argue, happened in Ahenakew's case.[2] Others countered that the airing of the words themselves is a harmful act, particularly in a broader social context of a rise of anti-Semitic activities in Canada.

In 1993, a lesbian magazine entitled *Bad Attitude* was found to breach the obscenity provisions of the *Criminal Code* and the Toronto store that sold it was fined for selling obscenity. The issue in question contained an article describing a sexual fantasy of domination and submission between two women. Experts testified at the trial that consensual domination and submission practices were well accepted within a particular subset of the lesbian community. However, the trial judge responded:

---

[1] R.S.C. 1985, c. C-46.
[2] See, for example, L.W. Sumner. *The Hateful and the Obscene: Studies in the Limits of Free Expression* (Toronto: University of Toronto Press, 2004).

> This material flashes every light and blows every whistle of obscenity. Enjoyable sex after subordination by bondage and physical abuse at the hands of a total stranger. If I replaced the aggressor in this article with a man there would be very few people in the community who would not recognize the potential for harm. The fact that the aggressor is a female is irrelevant because the potential for harm remains.[3]

The 'zine came to light because a conservative activist had gone into the store looking for materials involving children and gay sex; she took the 'zine to the Toronto police's anti-porn division (the P-Squad) and they laid the charges. GLBT groups around the world roundly condemned the decision as one curtailing freedom of expression of a minority community, asserting that fantasy literature was harmless, noting that the sex of the participants always makes a difference to sexual relations, and arguing that the actions revealed that Toronto police were actively pursuing minority communities through obscenity legislation, under the guise of enforcing the views of "the community".

As was noted in Chapter 1, the right of freedom of expression not only protects erudite or artistic forms of communication; it equally protects the offensive, the rude, the graphic. It protects expression that members of the mainstream would never read or view and that would offend them. However, all communities have their limits and some forms of expression can go too far for some. Where that line should be drawn has been at the heart of disputes about William Burroughs' book *Naked Lunch*, James Joyce's *Ulysses*, Vladmiri Nabokov's *Lolita*, Bernardo Bertolucci's film *Last Tango in Paris*, Robert Maplethorpe's and Eli Langer's paintings, or the music of Marilyn Manson and Lady Gaga. Regardless of how these disputes resolve legally, they all confirm our recognition of the power of expression to redraw community boundaries, to harm us, to move us (be that negatively or positively).

Expression is intimately connected with the production and communication of individual and group identity, both mainstream and minority. Expression is, therefore, one of the central means by which community is formed and reproduced. At the same time, rarely are all forms of expression acceptable to members of all groups or communities and those norms of acceptability change over time. This chapter examines some of the zones of contestation around the limits of acceptable expression. In a sense, it marks one of the ways in which we limit our expression in order to make our society work.

During and after disputes like those noted above, claims of censorship are often made. Censorship is generally understood as a term of

---

[3] *R. v. Scythes*, [1993] O.J. No. 537 at para. 9 (Ont. Prov. Div.).

censure indicating an activity which automatically offends freedom of expression. And yet, in Canadian society, we regularly censor. We take what might seem like the extreme step of criminalizing some forms of expression, and we do so on the basis of the understanding that expression, itself, can cause social and individual harm. Some expression, we feel, should be curtailed in the public interest. These limits, therefore, are important markers of how we define Canadian society, and how individuals and groups within Canadian society define themselves. They are a significant mechanism through which we negotiate social norms, and they are never simple and uncontested. The most significant forms of criminalized expression in Canada are known as obscenity and hate speech.

II. OBSCENITY

Sexual content in cultural production has historically been one of the most frequent means through which majority sensibilities, specific creators and communities, the state, the media, and the law have come into conflict and interaction. Sex serves as a measure to help define the limits of community in any given society. But as Dean Jobb notes, "what the community will tolerate is a moving target".[4] While *Lady Chatterley's Lover* might have been considered obscene in the late 1950s and early 1960s, 50 years later, no one would give it a second thought. There has been a "mainstreaming" of sorts of many forms of sexually explicit cultural content with a booming industry in "soft core" pornography.

Obscene communication is illegal in Canada and has been since the late 1800s. The current legislation was first established in 1959 and shifted the test for whether something was obscene from whether it had the tendency to corrupt public morals — the test from the late 1800s until the 1950s — to the "undue exploitation of sex". The 1959 legislation was passed, in part to attempt to stem the tide of mass market pulp fiction and magazines that swept Canada in the 1950s. This dynamic of the interplay between attempts to legislate in the area of obscenity and surges in the pornography industry, would repeat itself several times in Canadian history.

Section 163(1) of the *Criminal Code* provides that anyone "who makes, prints, publishes, distributes, circulates, or has in his possession for the purpose of publication, distribution or circulation any

---

[4]   Jobb, Dean. *Media Law for Canadian Journalists* (Toronto: Emond Montgomery Publications, Ltd., 2006) at 326.

obscene written matter, picture, model, phonograph record or other thing whatever" commits a criminal offence.[5] Further it is also an offence for anyone who "sells, exposes to public view or has in his possession for such a purpose any obscene written matter, picture, model, phonograph record or other thing whatever."[6] Thus, mere possession of obscene material is permitted, but any intention or action to make or distribute that communication more broadly (in any way) is prohibited. An obscene publication is defined as "any publication a dominant characteristic of which is the undue exploitation of sex, or of sex and any one or more of the following subjects, namely crime, horror, cruelty and violence".[7] A defence is provided for communications in "the public good" which is meant to provide exceptions for works with literary or other artistic merit.

In the early cases considering the 1959 legislation, interpretive benchmarks were established that still shape Canadian obscenity law. First, the element in the representation claimed to be obscene must be interpreted in the context of the work as a whole, and not considered in isolation. Second, the proper test for what constitutes "undue" should be the standards of acceptance that prevail in the community. It is not intended to be a measure of personal or subjective taste. The standard must be contemporary, namely, able to shift with the times and the community to be assessed is the nation as a whole. One asks, what will the Canadian community tolerate? Justice Dickson (as he then was) framed the test in these terms: "What matters is not what Canadians think is right for themselves to see. What matters is what Canadians would not abide other Canadians seeing because it would be beyond the contemporary Canadian standards of tolerance to allow them to see it."[8] These decisions begged the question, though: what is the Canadian community and how can we know it? Expert evidence as to what the national community standards were was understood to be desirable, although not essential.

There were attempts to revise the obscenity legislation over the mid- to late-1980s, in part as a result of the explosion of video pornography being imported, produced, sold and rented in Canada with the rise of video technology in the 1970s. Many courts had begun to signal greater tolerance for general sexual content in various media, although the standards by which this was assessed were quite different across the country as the case law from different regions reveals. Obscenity prosecutions began to decline because of the uncertainty in the interpretation

---

5   I am using the current section numbers for ease of interpretation.
6   Section 163(2).
7   Section 163(8).
8   *R. v. Towne Cinema Theatres Ltd.*, [1985] S.C.J. No. 24, [1985] 1 S.C.R. 494 at 508 (S.C.C.).

of the law and anti-pornography groups began to lobby government forcefully. Between 1977 and 1983, 40 bills addressing pornography were presented in Parliament, many of which were private members' bills seeking to tighten the strictures defining pornographic material. In January 1983 the CRTC granted licences to several pay-television stations showing sexually explicit visual content — the cries for action in some quarters grew louder.

In 1983, the government appointed the Fraser Committee — the Committee on Pornography and Prostitution — charged with evaluating the state of the law in both the areas of pornography and prostitution. It was to conduct cross-country hearings in order to work towards a national consensus that could inform policy-making. Its report generally reflected an anti-pornography perspective, but one informed by a particular feminist position which focused on pornography's detrimental impact upon women. While the Committee conceded that it was valuable to distinguish between pornography and erotica, it refused to define pornography given that there was no community consensus on what it should mean and what its limits should be. The Report recommended a complete overhaul of the existing legislative framework regulating pornography and child pornography. Interestingly, while recommending stronger criminal laws, the Fraser Report acknowledged that law was not the favoured means to deal with the issues raised by pornography and that only one per cent of the Canadian public was actually concerned about the issue to a significant degree.

The Conservative government proposed amendments to the *Criminal Code* in Bill C-114 in 1986 and went even further than the recommendations of the Fraser Committee. Rather than obscenity being determined by a standard set out in the Act, this legislation proposed to define pornography, itself, and did so very broadly to include any visual or textual material containing, among other things, "sexual intercourse" and "any other sexual activity". The legislation was met with stiff criticism from many avenues: civil libertarians, the media, feminist groups against censorship, some women's groups, artists' groups and others were all concerned that the bill focused on prohibiting the representation of sex, rather than of violence. Of particular concern was the inclusion of "other sexual activity" in the definition of pornography which would seem to preclude any representations of sexual activity whatsoever. The legislation died on the order paper at the parliamentary summer recess.

The government tried again in 1987 with Bill C-54 in what was clearly compromise legislation. It legalized "erotica" and criminalized pornography, largely in line with the recommendations of the Fraser Report, but continued to prohibit the representation of vaginal, anal or oral sexual intercourse, lactation, menstruation or ejaculation. Again artists' groups, civil libertarians, anti-censorship feminist groups and so on roundly critiqued it. Internationally renowned author, Pierre Burton, suggested it would make Canada the laughing stock of the Western World.[9] This time even library boards got into the game, criticizing the legislation to the point where the government declined to force the bill to a vote; the legislation again died on the order paper in the fall of 1988 when Parliament dissolved for an election. A political compromise seemed impossible and the obscenity provisions remained as they were. It was the Supreme Court of Canada that ultimately clarified what constitutes criminal obscenity in Canada in its watershed decision of *R. v. Butler*.[10]

Donald Butler ran a sexual paraphernalia shop in Winnipeg which also rented and sold sexually explicit videos and magazines. He was charged with a total of 250 counts of possessing and selling obscene material, as well as exposing obscene material to the public, as a result of the videos in particular. He argued that the *Criminal Code* was illegally restricting his freedom of expression under the *Canadian Charter of Rights and Freedoms*[11] and challenged the constitutionality of section 163(8). The trial judge convicted Butler with respect to eight specific films by virtue of their violent nature, finding the remainder of the content protected by section 2(b) of the *Charter*. The Crown appealed and the Manitoba Court of Appeal, in a split decision, allowed the Crown's appeal and convicted on all counts, holding that the films fell outside of freedom of expression completely and thus were not protected at all.

The first issue for the Supreme Court, then, was whether or not the pornographic videotapes even constituted expression within the meaning of section 2(b) of the *Charter*. Recall that the threshold is low for what constitutes expression with the communication in question merely having to convey meaning. The Manitoba Court of Appeal had held that the pornographic videotapes were not an attempt to convey meaning because they contained nothing but a series of physical acts devoid of intellectual content. The Supreme Court of Canada disagreed and stated that even if the content was distasteful, it was still expression within the meaning of the *Charter*.

Then further to the Oakes test, the issue became whether or not the provisions in the *Criminal Code* were a reasonable limit in a free and democratic society. The Court divided pornography into three different categories:

---

[9] In Danny Lacombe. *Blue Politics: Pornography and the Law in the Age of Feminism* (Toronto: University of Toronto Press, 1994) at 118.

[10] *R. v. Butler*, [1992] S.C.J. No. 15, [1992] 1 S.C.R. 452 (S.C.C.).

[11] Part I of *The Constitution Act*, being Schedule B to the *Canada Act 1982* (U.K.), 1982, c. 11.

1. explicit sex with violence;
2. explicit sex without violence, but which subjects people to treatment that is degrading and dehumanizing; and
3. explicit sex without violence that is neither degrading nor dehumanizing.

The Court found that it is likely that the first type of pornography will always be an undue exploitation of sex and thus fall within the expression prohibited by section 163; the second type of sexually explicit expression can be undue if the risk of harm from it is substantial; and the third type of sexually explicit material will not constitute an undue exploitation of sex unless children are used in its production.

In its effort to develop a test for obscenity that added to that of community standards of tolerance, the Court seized upon the notion of harm. The test offered up by the Court for whether or not something is obscene asks: does harm result from the expression? It does not matter if the work is extremely distasteful to many viewers. As well, the Court confirmed that sexually explicit work must be interpreted in its context. For example, it does matter if something is artistic. The court will ask if there are redeeming features to the expression — is it educational? It is the community which is the arbiter of what is harmful to it — in this case, the national community. It is the community's standard of tolerance that will determine the issue of harm. The court will therefore ask: would this expression exceed the tolerance of Canadians for what they think is harmful? The test for artistic merit is also one of the national community, not of an objective measure of artistry. No evidence is necessary for the community standards test for either harm or artistic merit although it can be tendered.

Recall that section 1 of the *Charter of Rights and Freedoms* permits reasonable limits to be placed on any right provided therein, including freedom of expression, provided that the limit is sanctioned by law and can be "demonstrably justified in a free and democratic society". Canada's highest Court in *Butler* held that the obscenity provisions, while a clear restriction on citizens' freedom of expression was "saved" by section 1 because the provisions were minimally invasive, and were intended to protect society more broadly, and women in particular, from harm. The Court took into account the attempts made in 1986 and 1988 to amend the obscenity legislation and their failure; the Court was aware that it would have been politically very difficult to replace the provisions with an amended version had they been struck down.

The argument about harm was somewhat controversial because as media scholars have repeatedly shown, it is very difficult to demonstrate direct harm caused by communicative means. Almost everyone studying the issue would concede that the viewing of mediated content does not leave us unchanged, particularly if the communication is extreme. However, exactly what the impact of that communication is on us, how it is produced and how it manifests is highly contested. Further, what the social causes are of sexism, misogyny and violence towards women are equally complex. The court concedes the harm need not be direct, but still requires a finding of harm in order to justify the infringement of freedom of expression. As a result, women's groups were split in their responses to the decisions. Groups strongly opposed to pornography, interpreting it on a continuum with other forms of violence towards women, applauded the decision and the framing of the issue as one of harm to women. In fact, American radical feminist Catherine MacKinnon had been a co-author of one of the briefs received by the Court and was overjoyed with the result in *Butler*. Other women's groups felt that the decision cast women in the roles of victims and still resulted in the treatment of sexual representation as a moral issue subject to the vagaries of majority opinion. Gay and lesbian freedom of expression advocates, in particular, were concerned about the impact of these provisions on non-mainstream sexual practices and representations — with good reason, as we shall see.

The *Butler* decision was generally recognized by all parties as a viable compromise, and certainly preferable to the abortive attempts at legislating the issue. Consumers of sexually explicit material could take some comfort from the categories generated by the Court as a means of determining, in advance, whether they were likely to be offending the legislative prohibitions. Certainly there have been fewer prosecutions regarding allegedly obscene material than in the pre-*Butler* era. However, as we shall see, there are still ongoing problems in the enforcement of the legislation.

III. CHILD PORNOGRAPHY

With the obscenity provisions having passed constitutional scrutiny, the nation's attention turned to child pornography when the Conservative government joined other Western nations and proposed Bill C-128 in the summer of 1993 — an amendment to the *Criminal Code* providing for restrictions on child pornography. The bill was passed very expeditiously with all party support despite loud concerns expressed by a number of arts and cultural groups, as well as civil libertarians, about the wording of the provisions and the extent of their potential reach. Many commentators felt that the legislation was unnecessary as child pornography was adequately covered within the existing obscenity provisions, when combined with *Butler*. Unlike the general obscenity provisions, rather than a measure of community tolerance, the child pornography provisions rely upon a description of content in order to define child pornography.

Section 163.1(1) of the *Criminal Code* defined child pornography as:

(a) a photographic, film, video or other visual representation, whether or not it was made by electronic or mechanical means,

(i) that shows a person who is or is depicted as being under the age of eighteen years and is engaged in or is depicted as engaged in explicit sexual activity, or

(ii) the dominant characteristic of which is the depiction, for a sexual purpose, or a sexual organ or the anal region of a person under the age of eighteen years; or

(b) any written material, visual representation or audio recording that advocates or counsels sexual activity with a person under the age of eighteen years that would be an offence under this Act.

The Act made it an offence to make, print, publish or possess for the purpose of publication child pornography, punishable by ten years' imprisonment. Anyone who transmitted, distributed, sold, imported, exported or possessed for the purpose of transmission, making available, distribution, sale or exportation child pornography was also committing an offence. Mere possession of child pornography was criminalized in section 163(4) and punishable by five years' imprisonment. As with the other obscenity provisions, there was a defence available in the original amendment if the material at issue has artistic merit or an educational, scientific or medical purpose.

The newly minted legislation was given its first test after a show of paintings and drawings exploring child sexuality by Eli Langer that opened at Toronto's Mercer Gallery in 1993. Two days after a negative review in the *Globe and Mail*, the Toronto police seized all of the art-works and arrested both the artist and the gallery's director. The charges were ultimately dropped against Langer and the director, but then the Ontario Crown applied for a forfeiture order to seize the paintings, which effectively required Langer to demonstrate that the paintings were not child pornography. He defended his artwork under the "artistic merit" defence built into the section, but also challenged the constitutionality of the child pornography provisions. The hearing was a dramatic affair and various artists testified in support of Langer that the works had "artistic merit" within the meaning of the *Criminal Code*. While the judge upheld the constitutionality of the child pornography provisions, he ultimately found that the works had artistic merit and that they should be returned to Langer. It was generally recognized that the P-squad had acted precipitously in their actions; however, this incident was the seeming instantiation of the worries of artists that these provisions would be used against them (something which the government had promised at the time would never happen). And while the artist ultimately prevailed, as Anne-Marie Kinehan points out, the decision reinforced the idea that the legal system was an appropriate venue for the determination of what constitutes art in our society.[12]

But this was not the end of the child pornography moral battle, nor of the struggles over artistic merit. This time, however, the defendant was less reputable and the results of the case were received quite differently. The child pornography provisions received their first constitutional challenge at the Supreme Court of Canada in the case of *R. v. Sharpe*.[13] John Robin Sharpe was a 65-year-old former community planner, a self-proclaimed advocate of inter-generational sex, and an admitted connoisseur of child pornography. Upon a raid of his apartment, police seized sexually explicit material involving children. Computer disks were seized from customs and books, manuscripts, stories and photographs were taken from his home. Some of the material featured actual children, other material consisted of journals and stories written by Sharpe and were fantasies. He opted to represent himself in court. The British Columbia Supreme Court dismissed the charges against him, holding that the *Criminal Code* provisions regarding mere possession were an undue violation of the accused's freedom of expression under the *Charter*. The British Columbia Court of Appeal upheld the decision, holding that making it an offence to merely possess material, when that material could have been produced without any harm to children and might never have been published, distributed or sold, was an extreme invasion of the accused's civil liberties. Accordingly, it found that section 163.1(4) was unconstitutional because it infringed freedom of expression and could not be saved by section 1 because the infringement was disproportional to the harm supposedly being remedied.

In 2001, the Supreme Court of Canada upheld the constitutional validity of section 163.1 in a unanimous decision. The Court rejected the claim that the imaginary nature of some of the content immediately placed it outside of the prohibition and held that the provision could apply to imaginary figures because the material could be harmful, even if they were not "real children". At the same time, however, it confirmed that freedom of expression extends to speech that the average person might find quite offensive and further, that the defence of artistic merit

---

12 Kinehan, Anne-Marie. "A Portrait of the Artist as a Sensitive Young Man: The State, the Media and 'The Ordeal' of Eli Langer" in *Pop Can: Popular Culture in Canada*, Lynne Van Luven and Priscilla L. Walton, eds. (Scarborough: Prentice Hall Allyn, 1999) 167 at 177.
13 [1999] B.C.J. No. 54, 169 D.L.R. (4th) 536 (B.C.S.C.), affd [1999] B.C.J. No. 1555, 175 D.L.R. (4th) 1 (B.C.C.A.), revd [2001] S.C.J. No. 3, [2001] 1 S.C.R. 45 (S.C.C.).

should be liberally construed. In its section 1 consideration, the Court held that child pornography posed a risk of harm to children and that the legislation was rationally connected to its prevention. The harm caused by child pornography was fourfold: first, it promotes cognitive distortion in its viewers/readers; second, it fuels fantasies that incite offenders to offend; third, it is used for grooming and seducing victims; and fourth, children are abused in making pornography that features real children.

In particular issue were the provisions criminalizing mere possession for private use. The Court accepted the argument that criminalizing possession may reduce the market for child pornography and as a result, reduce the abuse of children. Rather than finding the possession provisions unconstitutional, the Court opted to read in two exceptions. Self-created expressive material that was privately produced and used by the producer only was exempt from being categorized as child pornography. This would include diaries, journals and so on. The second form of exempted material were private recordings of legal sexual activity — photographs, video or sound — if taken by a minor for his or her own use.

The Court was also required to determine whether or not any of the material that was created by Sharpe fell within the exception provided for materials with artistic merit. Artistic merit, the Court held, would not be evaluated by community standards as was the case with adult obscene material, but by an objective standard of having either artistic character or artistic value. The test is essentially whether it is an expression that can be reasonably viewed as art. Expert testimony can be received by a court as to whether or not something has artistic merit.

The legislation having survived its constitutional challenge, Sharpe returned to Vancouver to stand trial on child pornography charges. Two of the charges pertained to photographs of boys in sexually explicit poses and he was convicted on those. However, the other charges pertained to Sharpe's own written work and on these, the trial judge held for the accused. He held that the work, while glorifying illegal activities, neither advocated nor counselled them within the meaning of the *Criminal Code*. Further, he accepted the argument that the works had artistic merit and were therefore exempted. Expert literary testimony was offered on Sharpe's work and it was split: two authors felt that it had artistic merit; two did not. The judge ultimately found that the stories did constitute an expression that might reasonably be viewed as art.

This decision was extremely controversial, and the political and media debates about the case took on a highly moralized tone. Artists groups, in particular, legitimately concerned about freedom of expression and artistic freedom, found themselves in the unenviable position of being cast as supporters of child pornography. It was much easier to defend the other side of the issue — protecting vulnerable children against pedophiles, perverts and pornographers. The House of Commons had even taken the highly unusual step of holding a vote to invoke what is known as "the notwithstanding clause" of the *Charter* to ensure that the law remained in force. The notwithstanding clause allows a government to specify that a statutory provision will remain in force despite a finding that it violates the *Charter of Right and Freedoms*. This initiative was defeated in the House by a vote of 143 to 129.

In order to address the seeming explosion of child pornography on the Internet, and as a result of concern with the *Sharpe* decision, the government specifically introduced Bill C-15A in 2001 which amended the *Criminal Code* to take account of online child pornography. Courts in Canada had already held that digital forms of child pornography were included in section 163.1 and that uploading files to a Bulletin Board System (BBS) that the public could access constituted distribution within the terms of the legislation. However, the Internet was widely recognized as having become the dominant medium for the circulation of child pornography given the difficulties law enforcement officials faced in locating and prosecuting offenders. Governments around the world felt the pressure to act. Canada's amendments came into force in 2002 and added the language of "transmission", "making available", and "accessing" to the distribution provisions. As well, subsections 163.1(4.1) and (4.2) were added making it an offence to knowingly "access" child pornography online.

However, further action was forthcoming from the government as it was not content with the substance of the *Sharpe* decision. As well, the Internet now became an element in the wider moral panic about child pornography that seemed to be sweeping the nation. Under the rubric of consulting the public about child victims, the federal government introduced Bill C-20 in 2002. A bill to protect children and other vulnerable persons from sexual exploitation, it expanded the definition of child pornography to include written material that describes sexual activity with minors. Therefore, the material no longer would need to "advocate or counsel" sexual activity, but merely express it. In other words, it lowered the standard from that against which Sharpe had been measured. As well, the artistic merit defence was changed to a defence involving the "public good". The legislation was criticized for its violation of freedom of expression, but unlike the critics of the obscenity provisions pertaining to adult sexual representations who could frame themselves as enlightened liberals, critics of increasing the scope of child pornography could be framed by opponents as advocating on behalf of Internet child pornographers. Nonetheless, the bill died on the order paper when Parliament was prorogued in late 2003.

The substance of Bill C-20 was reintroduced as Bill C-12 in early 2004. It faced similar criticism to its predecessor, particularly from artists' groups. That legislation, too, died on the order paper. However, it was reborn in the form of Bill C-2 which expanded child pornography offences, created a new prohibition against advertising child pornography, and replaced the "artistic" merit defence with that of "legitimate purpose". This legislation finally became law in 2005. The definition of child pornography was expanded to include audio material, as well as written material, the "dominant characteristic" of which is the description for a sexual purpose of sexual activity involving a minor that would be an offence under the *Code*. The work does not need to advocate or counsel such sexual activity. This means that if the *Sharpe* case were decided today, he likely would have been found guilty of possessing child pornography with respect to the written material which the Court found at the time did not "actively induce" offences with children.

Artists are left with the meagre solace of the revised section 163.1(6) of the *Criminal Code* which provides that:

> No person shall be convicted of an offence under this section if the act that is alleged to constitute the offence
>
> > (a) has a legitimate purpose related to the administration of justice or to science, medicine, education or art; and
> >
> > (b) does not pose an undue risk of harm to persons under the age of eighteen years.

While concerns remain that the provisions are an undue limitation on the right of freedom of expression contained in section 2(b) of the *Charter*, only future challenges in the courts will determine that issue. The legislation is subject to review by a parliamentary committee five years after coming into force.

IV. CRIMINALIZED EXPRESSION AND COMMUNITY

Just as artists had rightfully worried about the child pornography provisions being used to silence their expression, gays and lesbians were rightfully concerned that the obscenity provisions might well be used to persecute them. Perhaps more than any other case in the criminalization of expression, the ongoing dispute between the Little Sisters Bookstore and Canadian Customs officials reveals the ways in which expression is tied to identity and the negotiation of the norms of acceptable expression define both national, but also other forms of, community.

Little Sisters Book and Art Emporium is a Vancouver bookstore specializing in books, magazines and other material for the GLBT community. It had to import much of its stock from the United States and, in 1985, Canadian Customs began what was to be a long pattern of seizing material at the border intended for Little Sisters on the basis that it was alleged to be obscene according to customs guidelines. By the end of December 1986, more than 600 books and magazines, many of which could be found in Vancouver public libraries, had been seized in that month alone. The store's owners felt compelled to appeal these decisions and make their ongoing struggles with customs officials public. They challenged the seizure of several issues of the magazine, *The Advocate*, but before the matter went to court, the Canadian government conceded that the magazine was not obscene and the case was closed. Meanwhile, regular seizures continued and there were a number of incidents of violence directed towards the store and its owners. In 1990, Little Sisters and the B.C. Civil Liberties Association launched a challenge pursuant, in part, to section 2(b) of the *Charter*, arguing that the authority of Canada Customs, as well as its practices, violated their freedom of expression. The suit was filed in 1990, but the trial was not heard until 1994, having been adjourned three times. When it happened, the trial ran for 40 days with numerous high-profile authors appearing on behalf of the bookstore.

The British Columbia Supreme Court found that Canada Customs had discriminated against Little Sisters and enforced the law with arbitrariness, inconsistency and "just plain foolishness"; however, the judge upheld the legislation providing their authority to conduct the seizures. An appeal was launched and the British Columbia Court of Appeal, in 1998, upheld the lower court's decision that the right of customs officials to determine what is and is not obscene was constitutional. The bookstore appealed again to the Supreme Court of Canada, which, in late 2000, upheld the British Columbia courts' decisions, finding that while Little Sisters had been improperly persecuted by customs officials and discriminated against repeatedly, the legislation itself was not unconstitutional. Thus Little Sisters was vindicated morally, but defeated legally.[14]

While the legal outcome of the case is important, there are also other interesting findings that emerge from the Little Sisters decision that speak to the issue of community and criminalized expression. The case recognized a distinction between erotica and obscene sexual expression, and asserted the right of the state to criminalize obscene sexual

---

[14] *Little Sisters Book and Art Emporium v. Canada (Minister of Justice)*, [1996] B.C.J. No. 71, 131 D.L.R. (4th) 486 (B.C.S.C.), affd [1998] B.C.J. No. 1507, 160 D.L.R. (4th) 385 (B.C.C.A.), vard [2000] S.C.J. No. 66, 193 D.L.R. (4th) 193 (S.C.C.).

expression when it constitutes pornography. However, the court formally recognized that gay and lesbian erotica is more important to the community identity of gays and lesbians than heterosexual erotica is to that of heterosexuals. Yet despite this difference, the Supreme Court stated that gay and lesbian erotica is not more likely to be obscene than heterosexual erotica and that there should not be two standards governing their evaluation. But what does clearly emerge is a recognition of multiple communities of identity in Canada produced, in part, through the boundaries of acceptable expression.

The court made several findings with respect to the gay and lesbian community in Canada: first, it confirmed that there indeed is one. The relationship of individual gays and lesbians within this community was not specified. Further, the gay and lesbian community in Canada was held to be "disadvantaged" as sexuality is a source of profound vulnerability. The Court accepted "experts" or representatives of the gay and lesbian community as witnesses, testifying to the experience of being gay or lesbian. Their testimony was not merely a description of individual experience, but could be generalized to others in the eyes of the Court. The Court made no distinction between gay and lesbian identity for the purposes of the case. As well, for the Court, there was both a gay and lesbian community and a Canadian community that are understood as exclusive of each other, at least to some extent. Thus, the Court was attempting to affirm the existence and value of a queer identity, but was not prepared to recognize a differential measure for obscenity within that community. It will still be the "Canadian community", presumably dominated by heterosexuals, that will determine what is or is not obscene. Thus, sexual expression in part defines the boundaries of certain communities, but whether or not that sexual expression is criminal and should be limited by the law is not to be determined by them. Here the law both affirmed homosexual modes of identity and limited their means of expressing themselves. As Lisa Bower notes, "[l]aw is thus fruitfully reconceived as a discourse that both 'fixes' identity and creates rhetorical and discursive conditions for contesting that identity in a public forum."[15]

V. HATE SPEECH

Equally controversially and emotionally loaded, but in very different ways, "hate speech" has also been criminalized in Canada. While generally perceived as a racially tolerant nation, Canada has not remained

---

[15] Bower, Lisa C. "Queer Acts and the Politics of 'Direct Address': Rethinking Law, Culture and Community" (1994) 28 (5) Law & Soc'y Rev. 1009 at 1019.

untouched by racism and violence against racial and ethnic minorities, nor has it been untouched by other forms of the persecution of minorities (as we saw in the violence and persecution directed repeatedly against the Little Sisters bookstore). Some have suggested that expression is central to the propagation of those ideas and violent activities and that it is therefore an appropriate site of state regulation and censorship. There are provisions in the *Criminal Code* prohibiting hate speech, as well as in the *Canadian Human Rights Act*,[16] and the provincial human rights codes in British Columbia, Alberta, Saskatchewan and the Northwest Territories. As well, recall from Chapter 1 that the federal regulations pertaining to broadcasting also prohibit comments and pictorial representations that will expose an identifiable group to hatred on a number of grounds. The focus of this section will be on the federal criminal provisions criminalizing hate speech.

In the wake of World War II and concerns about the rise of neo-Nazism, the Canadian government created the Special Committee on Hate Propaganda (known as the Cohen Committee), which reported to Parliament in 1966.[17] The hate speech provisions were first added to the *Criminal Code* in 1970 in response to the Cohen Committee's report which claimed that hate propaganda posed a clear and present danger to Canadian democracy and values. Interestingly, Bill C-250 did not go through Senate hearings and it passed by a margin of 89 to 45 votes in the House of Commons, with 127 Members of Parliament absent or not voting. In so doing, Canada distinguished itself from many Western nations in its criminalization of hate speech and many legal and social commentators, while by no means advocating hate speech, have deep concerns about the legislation and its effect on political speech in Canada.

Section 318 of the *Criminal Code* prohibits the advocacy or promotion of genocide in either private or public communication. Section 319(1) prohibits the public communication of statements that might incite hatred against any identifiable group, where such incitements are likely to lead to a breach of the peace and the communication of statements, other than private conversations, that willfully promote hatred against any identifiable group. Additionally, section 319(2) prohibits public communication willfully promoting hatred against an identifiable group, whether or not violence ensues, although prosecutions cannot be brought under this section without the consent of the Attorney General of the relevant province. "Identifiable group" means any group identified by colour, race, religion, ethnic origin or sexual orientation. Again, there

---

[16] R.S.C. 1985, c. H-6.

[17] Cohen Committee, *Report to the Minister of Justice of the Special Committee on Hate Propaganda in Canada* (Ottawa: Queen's Printer, 1966).

are four defences provided within the legislation that apply to section 319(2) given its capacity to infringe freedom of expression. First, if the facts stated can be demonstrated to be true or if the accused's belief in their truth is based upon reasonable grounds, then he or she will be acquitted. Second, if the statements are made in good faith as part of a discussion of religion, they are not hate speech. Third, if the statements are relevant to the public interest and the accused reasonably believed them to be true, then an exception is provided. Fourth and finally, the speech will not breach the section if it is uttered by a speaker attempting to have the speech removed from public circulation.

Section 319(2) has been one of the most contentious provisions for those advocating free speech and opposed to government censorship of what they claim to be political speech, no matter how vile. There have been very few prosecutions brought pursuant to section 319 and even fewer convictions. Not surprisingly, these provisions were open to a *Charter* challenge that they unduly violated freedom of expression. The first and most significant test of the legislation to date came in the case of *R. v. Keegstra*. James Keegstra was a high school teacher in Alberta who was advocating anti-Semitic views to his students in the classroom. He suggested that Jews were evil; they were seeking to destroy Christianity, were responsible for economic depressions, anarchy, chaos, wars, and revolutions and had invented the Holocaust in a bid for international sympathy. If students did not reproduce his views, their grades suffered. When this came to light, he was fired from his job and charged under section 319(2) (then 281.2(2)) of the *Criminal Code*.

Keegstra initially made an application to have the charge quashed because it violated section 2(b) of the *Charter*. That failed and he was convicted at trial, where the freedom of expression argument failed again. It succeeded, however, at the Alberta Court of Appeal where that Court overturned his conviction and found that the hate speech provisions were unconstitutional, not meeting the section 1 justification. The Crown appealed to the Supreme Court of Canada which released its split decision in 1990. All of the judges agreed that the hate speech provisions of the *Criminal Code* violated freedom of expression, but they differed on whether or not they could be justified under section 1. All felt that there was a sufficiently pressing need, but they differed on the proportionality test. The dissent argued that the legislation failed both the rational connection and minimal impairment requirements. Justice McLachlin argued that prosecuting hate mongers can give them a further platform for their views and sometimes garner them public sympathy. Similar legislation had not been successful in combating racism in other jurisdictions. Because "hatred" was such a broad notion, it could have a chilling effect on freedom of expression and there were non-criminal means to pursue the issue, such as human rights provisions. The majority, on the other hand, argued that prosecuting hate mongers can have positive symbolic effects and that hatred should be strictly interpreted. "Hatred" was clarified and defined as "an emotion of an intense and extreme nature that is clearly associated with vilification and detestation".[18] The Court held that hatred, "implies that those individuals are to be despised, scorned, denied respect and made subject to ill-treatment on the basis of group affiliation".[19]

The Court confirmed that while freedom of expression is fundamental to the operation of a free and democratic society, limits on expression are also reasonable and justified in that society. It was recognized that the use of the criminal law to prohibit these types of communication signifies the public's contempt for hate speech. Speech which was hateful was held by the majority to be some distance from the kinds of speech intended to be supported within section 2(b). Similarly to the *Butler* decision, the section 1 argument was made in relation to an argument about the harm that is done by this type of expression. The Court claimed that it offends an individual's sense of her dignity and can have grave psychological and social consequences for its target. As well, hate speech hurts broader society because it may lead to violence and discrimination. The limits posed by the hate speech provisions were found to be reasonable limits on freedom of expression in a free and democratic society and Keegstra's conviction was upheld.

The approach of the Canadian legislatures and courts towards hate speech is very different than that taken by the United States. Similar legislative provisions to sections 318 and 319 of the Canadian *Criminal Code* would undoubtedly fall afoul of the free speech guarantee in the First Amendment of the American Constitution. The majority in *Keegstra* was aware of this difference and addressed it directly:

> Where s. 1 operates to accentuate a uniquely Canadian vision of a free and democratic society, however, we must not hesitate to depart from the path taken in the United States. Far from requiring a less solicitous protection of *Charter* rights and freedoms, such independence of vision protects these rights and freedoms in a different way. … [I]n my view the international commitment to eradicate hate propaganda and, most importantly, the special role given equality and multiculturalism in the Canadian Constitution necessitate a departure from the view, reasonably prevalent in America at present, that the suppression of hate propaganda is incompatible with the guarantee of free expression.[20]

18
   R. v. Keegstra, [1990] S.C.J. No. 131, [1990] 3 S.C.R. 697 at para. 116 (S.C.C.).
19
   Ibid.
20
   Ibid., at para. 56.

At the same time that the Supreme Court released its decision in *Keegstra*, it also released its decision in *CHRC v. Taylor*[21] and upheld the constitutionality of the hate speech provisions in the *Canadian Human Rights Act*, similarly a split decision.

Another high profile case that pitted freedom of expression against criminal speech was the attempt to prosecute Holocaust denier Ernst Zundel. He was charged by Canadian police after he published a booklet entitled, "Did Six Million Really Die?" While the booklet had been previously published in both Britain and the United States, Zundel wrote a new foreword and postscript for the Canadian edition. In it, he argued that evidence did not substantiate that six million Jewish people were killed during World War II, and that the Holocaust was a myth perpetuated by an international Jewish conspiracy. Zundel was convicted at both his trial and his retrial. The appeal to the Supreme Court of Canada was from his conviction at the second trial.

While also a case on the criminalizing of expression, the key difference between the *Keegstra* and *Zundel* decisions, however, is that Zundel was charged under section 181 of the *Criminal Code*, which provided that: "Every one who wilfully publishes a statement, tale or news that he knows is false and that causes or is likely to cause injury or mischief to a public interest is guilty of an indictable offence and liable to imprisonment for a term not exceeding two years." The majority decision was very clear that this case was not about hate speech as that is defined in the *Criminal Code*; rather it was about the making of false statements that caused injury or mischief to a public interest, a much vaguer and broader charge.

The Supreme Court held that section 181 did infringe section 2(b) of the *Charter* and could not be repudiated by section 1. As with all cases involving offensive communication, the Court reaffirmed that all communications that convey or attempt to convey meaning are protected by section 2, unless the media of communication itself is prohibited, for example, through violence. The meaning of the text and its general offensiveness are not relevant to whether or not it merits protection. And while the communications in this instance were highly offensive, they were still protected by section 2(b). However, when the Court applied the section 1 test, the provision failed. More specifically, the objective of the legislation was found to be neither pressing nor substantial. The section was anachronistic and the falsity of the message did not go to its constitutionality. The Court suggested that there might well be value in certain false statements. In fact, it was, in large part, the contrast between the much more specific provisions of sections 318 and 319, clearly addressing hate speech and the much more vague provisions of section 181 that

---

[21] [1990] S.C.J. No. 129, [1990] 3 S.C.R. 892 (S.C.C.).

were ultimately the latter's undoing. There was no pressing need for solving the problem at the heart of section 181 and the Court recognized that the Law Reform Commission had recommended its abolition in its 1986 report, *Working Paper 50: Hate Propaganda*. So the resolution was, by no means, a vindication of Zundel, nor was it a rejection of the principle of criminalizing hate speech in Canada, it was merely that the legal provision in question was outdated and unnecessary in light of the more recent hate speech provisions.

As with obscenity, and in particular, child pornography, the Internet has become a virtual haven for various individuals engaging in forms of expression that might fall within the Canadian definition of hate speech. As a medium, it is inexpensive, accessible by millions, is used by young people in particular, and poses difficult jurisdictional challenges to authorities. Hate sites can often operate under the radar because unless one is looking specifically for them, one is unlikely to encounter them. In other words, the level of general scrutiny is low. As a result of these factors, Jane Bailey has rightly claimed that the Internet has become the preferred location for hate mongers.[22] Again, governments around the world felt called upon to take some sort of action against the explosion of online hate sites.

In Canada, that action took the form of further legislation. Section 320 of the *Criminal Code* had always prohibited the distribution and sale of hate propaganda, but in 2001 the Canadian government extended that power expressly to the Internet as part of its response to the attacks of 9-11 in the *Anti-Terrorism Act*.[23] In section 320.1, a judge has the authority to order an ISP to remove hate speech from a computer system in Canada that is accessible to the public, as well as to provide the necessary information to the court to identify the person who posted the material. The judge can make this order regardless of whether or not a prosecution is taking place under section 319 and there is no requirement of "willfully" promoting hatred in section 320. To date this section has been evoked extremely rarely.[24]

Most ISPs have "acceptable use" policies that they have developed in order to give them the grounds to intervene in hate-mongering sites. This was the basis upon which a Canadian ISP recently removed the "Realjewnews.com" from its server, once it was alerted by a Jewish anti-hate research group and had reviewed the content. Within days, however,

---

[22] Bailey, Jane. "Private Regulation and Public Policy: Toward Effective Restriction of Internet Hate Propaganda" (2004) 49 McGill L. J. 59 at para. 1.

[23] S.C. 2001, c. 41.

[24] Slane, Andrea. "Combatting Hate on the Internet: Current Canadian Efforts and the Recommendations of Non-Governmental Organizations to Improve on Them", Working Paper for the Department of Justice Canada (2007), at 44, claims that 320.1 was used only once.

the site had reappeared, this time in another legal jurisdiction. This highlights the challenge that those wishing to prosecute online hate speech through legislation face. It is safe to say that there is no international consensus on how best to combat hate speech, on- or off-line, although once again, as in the other areas we have taken up, Canada is pursuing its own unique path.

VI. CONCLUSION

The Canadian state and courts have recognized the power of expression not only to enlighten and inform, as we have seen in previous chapters, but also to offend and harm. When it harms, that expression is a criminal activity. These strictures necessarily and deliberately offend the freedom of expression. We have seen from the legislative struggles and disputes in each of the three areas of criminalized speech — obscenity, child pornography and hate speech — that negotiating those boundaries through the political process is an ongoing challenge. This difficulty has contributed to a fairly high level of judicial deference being paid to the provisions of the *Criminal Code* pertaining to expression. Rather than finding the legislation unconstitutional, as an unjustified infringement of freedom of expression, the courts have preferred to add layers of specificity to the pertinent definitions and standards and to read in additional exceptions. In this way, the Supreme Court of Canada is taking a more restrained approach to freedom of expression than it has in relation to the other areas explored in this text.

Although hopefully most of us will not have a direct encounter with the limitations that criminalizing hate speech places on our right to freedom of expression, it is a measure of the political culture of Canada as a nation. In this, as well as in the areas of its obscenity and child pornography provisions, Canada has some of the strictest limits on free expression in the Western world. It marks us as a nation which advocates censorship over the approach of contesting offensive speech in the public sphere, as the United States prefers. Whether this is a good or a bad choice on the part of Parliament is a question that is open for debate. That debate itself is important because it is through it that we define the distinction between art and obscenity, between deviant and marginal, between mainstream and minority. Through the debates surrounding criminalized expression, we define the boundaries of "national community", the identities of members of minority communities, and mark what kinds of speech (and hence which speakers) are inside and outside of those multiple communities.

Chapter 5

Mediating the Law: Telling Legal Stories

I. INTRODUCTION

The defendants in a recent Arkansas trial were ordered to pay a $12.6 million judgement but have applied for a mistrial. While in the courtroom, juror Jonathan Powell began to "tweet" on his cellphone. (A Tweet is a web posting that is limited to 140 characters that can be sent and received on a mobile phone or computer). Powell's tweets included: "So Jonathan what did you do today? Oh nothing really, I just gave away TWELVE MILLION DOLLARS of someone else's money" and "Oh and nobody by Stoam. It's bad mojo and they'll probably cease to exist now they're wallet is 12m lighter." He insists that he only sent the messages after the verdict in the trial was announced, but the matter is being investigated.

In a large federal drug trial in Florida in 2009, a juror admitted to the presiding judge, after eight weeks of testimony, that he had been researching the case on the Web during his breaks. Upon inquiring further, the judge discovered that eight other jurors had done the same thing. Because it is a hallmark of American justice that jurors make their decisions based only on the evidence presented in the courtroom by the parties, the judge had no choice but to declare what has been dubbed by journalists, the first ever "Google mistrial".

Judge William E. Baldwin, in a recent murder trial in Shenandoah, specifically directed the jury not to watch that Wednesday's episode of *Law and Order*. The episode featured three highschool basketball players charged with killing an illegal immigrant. In the real life trial, three teenage boys were charged with yelling racial slurs at their victim and then beating him to death. The judge said to the jury, "I don't think it's an accident they're airing it this week. You may not watch it."

These are three interesting examples of only some of the myriad ways in which communications technologies are impacting upon the administration of justice and how everyday citizens understand the law. In the first example, the juror was using technology to circulate information to the public that was to remain in the courtroom. In the second, the jury member was using communications technology to bring external information into the courtroom that was not certified by the adversarial process as legitimate evidence. And in the third, the jurors were being told not to access media technology because of the fictional narrative it was transmitting, and the impact that might have on them.

This chapter takes up the ways that law expresses itself to the public through communications technologies and the corresponding relationship of the public with legal knowledge. As noted earlier, most Canadians do not regularly read the decisions of the Supreme Court of Canada online or walk to their local law library to peruse the consolidated statutes of their province. On the other hand, they do watch the evening television news, they do listen to the radio news in their cars, and they do watch *Law and Order: Special Victims Unit* and *The Practice*. Most of us feel that we have a general knowledge of the laws of our country and how they operate, even though most of us have not studied in law school. And we would probably be right. In part because not only is the law all around us, but stories about the law are all around us. In part because there is a productive relationship between media institutions, technologies of communication, and the public's knowledge of law. This chapter takes up that relationship and the ways in which we tell ourselves stories about the law.

While this chapter explores the mediation of the law, unlike Chapter 2, where the focus was on the legal constraints faced by journalists in relation to what information they can provide to the public and when, this chapter examines *how* the law is mediated. In the first section, we will examine the ways in which media technologies themselves (about which the courts have had a high level of concern), have been permeating the courtroom environment in a variety of ways. We will see the clash of values in the defence of the proper administration of justice and decorum in the courtroom with the call for greater transparency in legal proceedings and the difficulties of creating technology-free zones in our current era of mobile communications technology. At the same time, courts and judges are increasingly sensitive to the fact that they have reputations to maintain and that sequestering themselves from public scrutiny and availability is not the best way to maintain their credibility in this highly mediated age. In the second section, we will turn to the ways in which law is represented — both in the news and in popular culture narratives. We will examine some of the structural challenges faced by media organizations in legal reporting, typical patterns that are evident in their coverage, and how information is communicated about the legal system to the average citizen. We will also consider how popular culture representations of law educate the public about general legal principles, but can, at the same time, contribute to distorting their understandings of the operational details of the legal system.

II. MEDIA TECHNOLOGY IN THE COURTROOM

The courts are public institutions. As discussed in Chapter 2, the right of public access to the courts is captured in what is called the "openness principle". This idea dates to at least the 1400s in England and holds that the public's capacity to scrutinize the justice system is integral to the operation of a healthy democratic society. Media, it is argued, act as the public's representatives in the exercise of this right. Various Supreme Court of Canada decisions have reiterated not only the applicability, but the centrality, of the openness principle in Canada both before and after the adoption of the *Canadian Charter of Rights and Freedoms*[1]. These decisions have also recognized the key role that media organizations and journalists play in the exercise of this right. For example, Madam Justice Wilson stated the rationale for the protection of the openness principle in the *Edmonton Journal* case in this way:

> [i]n summary, the public interest in open trials and in the ability of the press to provide complete reports of what takes place in the court-room is rooted in the need (1) to maintain an effective evidentiary process; (2) to ensure a judiciary and juries that behave fairly and that are sensitive to the values espoused by the society; (3) to promote a shared sense that our courts operate with integrity and dispense justice; and (4) to provide an ongoing opportunity for the community to learn how the justice operates and how the law being applied daily in the courts affects them.[2]

Clearly, since the advent of the still camera, journalists have been using communications technology, in this case visual, to enhance or even replace traditional forms of text-based reporting. Journalism as a profes-sional practice has changed very dramatically in the last one 100 years and it is now fully multimedia. Not so with the courts. The courts in Canada, in particular, have historically been very "camera shy". This despite the fact that many would argue that in a media society, the use of cameras would be one of the most effective ways to embody the openness principle.

There are prohibitions on still photography, videocameras and broad-casting in most Canadian jurisdictions, although these take differing forms. Ontario is the only province that has legislative provisions specifically prohibiting the use of cameras in the courts. Section 136(1) of the *Courts of Justice Act*[3] is quite broad and provides:

---

[1] Part I of *The Constitution Act*, being Schedule B to the *Canada Act 1982* (U.K.), 1982, c. 11.
[2] *Edmonton Journal v. Alberta (A.G.)*, [1989] S.C.J. No. 124, [1989] 2 S.C.R. 1326 (S.C.C.).
[3] R.S.O. 1990, c. C.43.

Subject to subsections (2) and (3), no person shall,

(a) take or attempt to take a photograph, motion picture, audio recording or other record capable of producing visual or aural representations by electronic means or otherwise,

   (i) at a court hearing,

   (ii) of any person entering or leaving the room in which a court hearing is to be or has been convened, or

   (iii) of any person in the building in which a court hearing is to be or has been convened where there is reasonable grounds for believing that the person is there for the purpose of attending or leaving the hearing;

(b) publish, broadcast, reproduce or otherwise disseminate a photograph, motion picture, audio recording or record taken in contravention of clause (a); or

(c) broadcast or reproduce an audio recording made as described in clause 2(b).

The exceptions allow people, in practice typically journalists, to take notes or make sketches in an unobtrusive manner or to make an audio recording where its sole purpose is to supplement note-taking. As well, the presiding judge may permit visual or aural recording where necessary for the conduct of the legal proceeding in question, in relation to a ceremonial or other similar purpose, or with the consent of the parties and witnesses for educational or instructional purposes.

In the other provinces, the power to prohibit recording devices in the courtroom stems from an overall power granted to judges to control their own courtrooms. For example, the *Rules of Practice of the Superior Court of Quebec*[4] provide:

> Anything that interferes with the decorum and good order of the court is prohibited. The reading of newspapers, the practice of photography, cinematography, broadcasting or television are equally prohibited during the sittings of the Court. Sound recording of the proceedings and of the decision, as the case may be, by the media, shall be permitted unless the judge decides otherwise. Such recording shall not be broadcast.

Recording is permitted, but broadcasting is not. Other provinces rely on the directive provided by the Attorney-General's office and the provincial Chief Justice to enforce an unwritten ban that exists in practice. In British Columbia, for example, it is the general policy of the Supreme Court to prohibit tape recorders in courtrooms, but they can be permitted

---

[4] *Code of Civil Procedure*, R.S.Q., c. C-25, a. 47.

by the judge if certain circumstances are met. As well, journalists can apply to a Provincial Court judge for permission to televise or broadcast all or part of a proceeding, and if the judge in question feels it is in the public interest and not injurious to the proceedings or the accused, he or she may grant the application. In Manitoba, journalists can use tape recorders for verification purposes without making an application, but they cannot broadcast those recordings. Nova Scotia permits cameras in the courtroom with the prior permission of the sitting judge.

There are strong arguments on both sides of the debate. Advocates of cameras in the courtroom suggest that it is in keeping with the openness principle, that it provides a valuable scrutiny of the legal system, and that it educates the public. They argue that, properly administered, there would be no necessary disruption of the decorum or efficient administration of the courtroom, and that it should not adversely affect the trial of the issue. They suggest that participants in the legal process "behave better" knowing that they are being surveilled and that it is useful for the public to see judges at work. A citizenry that is well informed about how the legal system in their country operates is a citizenry that has more respect for its legal institutions, they claim. They also point out that television is the primary source of news for Canadians, suggesting that if the legal system wants a well-informed public, it should look to permitting the broadcast of legal cases. A videotape of a proceeding is also a complete record which can be used by the court itself, but also by lawyers and scholars, in their work. Finally, they argue there is little to no substantive and credible scientific evidence suggesting any negative impacts on the legal process as a result of mediated access. The American experience with cameras in courtrooms generally supports this position. In further support of their position, they point to Canada's own experience with televising over 80 public inquiries, concerning a variety of issues — some quite controversial — which is generally believed not to have had a detrimental impact upon those proceedings.

Those opposed to media technology in the courtroom worry about the possibilities of the "media circus" and its impact on the proceedings and the rights of the participants. They claim that almost all participants in the legal process can be negatively affected by the presence of cameras — witnesses can be intimidated and put in danger, defendants can have their privacy invaded, lawyers may start grandstanding, and jurors can receive information which is not proper evidence. Opponents claim that the public is not automatically well-served by the information they will receive through broadcasts, that these may in fact provide a distorted view of the law, and that the process risks turning justice into entertainment. For example, they would be concerned that the manner of television reporting — brief segments that are highly visualized with little context — do not lend themselves to adequately informing viewers about the complexities of legal issues. The space of the courtroom itself can be negatively affected in managing the presence of cameras. Concerns are often expressed about the additional costs associated with televising trials, such as adapting courtrooms and increased costs for sequestering juries if there are concerns about them being tainted by non-evidentiary information. Finally, the most commonly voiced concern is that using media technology for direct transmission of trials out of a courtroom risks bringing the administration of justice into disrepute.

Those are the arguments, in principle, but what has been happening in practice? Unlike Canada, where cameras are still the exception, in the United States, they are the norm in all states, but are prohibited in all federal courtrooms during criminal trials. James M. Linton points out that this was not always the case, but the move towards televising legal proceedings took place over the 1970s.[5] In 1991, this culminated in *Court TV*, a 24-hour television network devoted to televising legal cases. There is extensive trial coverage and proceedings are explained to viewers by lawyers and law professors. It has been wildly popular and has spawned imitators in Canada and the United States. At the same time, the televised trials of O.J. Simpson, the Menendez brothers, Lorena Bobbit, and W. Kennedy-Smith turned into full-on media spectacles and led to resulting criticisms of how coverage was managed in those instances. The spectre of these cautionary tales of American excess seemingly hang over the Canadian decision-makers.

Canadian courts have historically been much more reluctant to permit the mediation of their courtrooms, with discussion and litigation of the issue only beginning in the 1980s. In the late 1980s, there were a series of regulatory bodies which recommended changes to the rules and practice norms excluding electronic media technologies from courtrooms. In 1987, the Law Reform Commission was charged with examining public and media access to the criminal justice system. Its final report was entitled *Public and Media Access to the Criminal Process*, and went so far as to recommend that electronic media coverage of criminal trials be permitted, that audio recordings be allowed in place of, or in addition to, handwritten notes, and that Canada ought to experiment for a significant period of time with the issue so that it might actually map the "effects" of electronic media coverage on the criminal trial process.[6] An Ontario judge charged with reviewing the Ontario court system generally,

---

[5]   Linton, James M. "Camera Access to Courtrooms: Canadian, U.S., and Australian Experiences" (1993) 18(1) Canadian Journal of Communication.

[6]   Law Reform Commission of Canada, *Working Paper 56* (Ottawa: Minister of Supply and Services Canada, 1987).

recommended that the province's laws be changed to provide for a two-year experiment allowing electronic communications technology into the courtrooms.[7] As well, the Canadian Bar Association (CBA) appointed a Special Committee on Cameras in the Courts, which reported in 1987 and led to a reversal of the CBA's previous position opposing mediated access. The CBA also recommended a two-year trial period for televisual and photographic media access.

An early experiment was in fact conducted in Ontario trial courts in 1982, catalyzed by the Radio Television News Directors Association of Canada under the supervision of the Chief Justice's Bench and Bar Committee. Trials and hearings were filmed and a number of episodes were broadcast on television featuring different aspects of the courts and the legal system. Members of the public indicated that it was informative and the judges and lawyers involved in the pilot project were very positive. Despite the success on all fronts of the experiment, judicial apathy seemed to set in and no changes were made to Ontario law or court practice. Despite the clear trend with most other actors in the legal and media systems towards some form of electronic media access to the courts, the Canadian Judicial Council (the umbrella group for Canadian judges) continues to this day to resist cameras in Canadian courtrooms. It did, however, soften its position with respect to the Supreme Court of Canada in the 1990s, and in 2002 exempted appellate courts from its position.

In 1992, the CBC decided to have a run at the constitutionality of the statutorily prescribed limits on broadcasting from a court. A CBC reporter named Cathy Squires was charged for directing a camera person to film someone leaving a courthouse. She acknowledged causing the photograph to be taken, but based her defence on her guarantee of freedom of expression. She argued that if she had the right to be in the courtroom, then she had the right to use whatever tools she, as a reporter, would use to do her job. After being convicted at trial and fined $500, the CBC launched an appeal to the Ontario Court of Appeal. There the 3 to 2 decision was that the laws prohibiting photographing, video and recording were constitutional. The Court conceded they were a limit on freedom of expression, but felt that the state had three legitimate justifications for these limits. First, the judge was entitled to maintain order and decorum in his or her courtroom. Second, it was important to guarantee unimpeded access to the courtroom. Third, and finally, the law guarantees a reasonable expectation of privacy on the part of the participants.

---

[7] Zuber, The Honourable T.G. *Report of the Ontario Courts Inquiry* (Toronto: Ministry of the Attorney General, 1987).

Despite some of the arguably problematic reasoning behind the decision, the Supreme Court declined to hear the appeal.

The courts in Canada have seemingly been reluctant to use the *Charter* as the basis for bringing media technology into the courtroom, preferring perhaps to allow the practices to change in a more tempered and gradual pace at the policy level instead. A number of requests to televise criminal trials in Canada have been denied by courts and challenged by media organizations, without success. Unfortunately, the courts in these cases have not offered detailed reasons or analysis of the issues. However, significant changes have taken place at the policy level over the course of the 1990s and the 2000s.

Interestingly, it is the Supreme Court of Canada which has led the way. In 1981 it broke new ground by permitting the broadcast of the *Patriation Reference* case where the legal capacity of Canada to patriate its own Constitution was referred to the Court. It permitted occasional broadcast of proceedings in 1983 and of a number of appeals over the 1990s, including the poignant case of Sue Rodriguez who was dying of Lou Gehrig's disease and fought for the right to have a physician assist her with her intended suicide without breaking the law. Since the mid-1990s, the Supreme Court has videotaped all of its cases, for its own use as well as for that of the media, lawyers and scholars. This adoption of media access was part of a larger shift in the relationship of Canada's highest court with the nation's media organizations which was catalyzed with the 1982 repatriation of the Constitution and the adoption of the *Charter of Rights and Freedoms*. With the adoption of the *Charter*, Canada adopted a system of constitutional supremacy which empowered the courts to sit in judgement of the legislation of the provincial and federal governments. The Supreme Court became a much more significant political player and as a result became subject to much greater media scrutiny. The Chief Justices since that time have recognized these developments with increasing efforts to open up the Court.

Since the 1980s, the Supreme Court has come a long way towards modernizing its attitude towards not only communications technology, but towards the idea of mediation more generally. While polls of the Canadian public repeatedly demonstrate a high level of public approval of the Supreme Court of Canada (indeed more than most other social institutions, including governments), the Court is not sitting on those laurels. It has seemingly recognized that its credibility is, in part, achieved, through the sense of that institution that Canadians derive from the media content they consume. As Florian Sauvageau *et al.*, note: "[t]he justices of the Supreme Court cannot hide behind a protective wall of distant and dignified authority. They must, in their own way, campaign for public favour."[8]

There are a number of initiatives that Canada's highest court has undertaken to demonstrate that it is a "media-friendly" and open public institution. The Court itself is physically open to the public, as it always has been, but now the schedule of hearings is online for easy consultation. There are a number of seats in the courtroom reserved for media personnel and simultaneous translation is provided to them. Audio recorders can be used, but individual cameras are not permitted. Journalists can use laptops and handheld devices like Blackberries (with the sound turned off) and there are electronic outlets and free wireless Internet service offered. There is also a Press Room which features a closed circuit television feed of the appeal in English and French as it is taking place. The Press Room also contains copies of the factums (the argumentation documents submitted by the parties and intervenors) for the use of journalists. A live feed of all appeals is provided to the Parliamentary Press Gallery, and since 1997, Canada's public affairs cable channel (CPAC) broadcasts them at a later date. Journalists can apply to the Court for permission to use photographs, video or webcasts under certain circumstances. Email is used by the Court to circulate press releases and notices about judgements, hearings and so on. When a cluster of high-profile decisions are to be released at the same time, the Court now staggers them over a two-day period so as to not overwhelm news agencies; it has also, in response to media pressures, regularized the timing of the release of decisions in a manner more compatible with the news cycle. As well, judges are much more accessible to the media, speaking in public more frequently and giving more interviews to the press (although never, of course, discussing a current case or debating reasons for past decisions). As well, in 1981, the Chief Justice of the day, Bora Laskin, created a media relations committee which continues to operate, meeting once or twice a year with the mandate to reflect on the mediation process and to deal with any complaints.

The most important change in the relationship between the Supreme Court and media organizations and journalists was the creation of the position of the Executive Legal Officer (ELO) in 1985 to serve as a liaison between the Court and the reporters covering it. The ELO is an independent expert who provides additional information, context and guidance to reporters who are having to receive, read, digest and summarize for the public often extremely complex decisions in very short amounts of time. The ELO is usually a trained lawyer and frequently an

---

[8] Sauvageau, Florian, David Schneiderman & David Taras. *The Last World: Media Coverage of the Supreme Court of Canada* (Vancouver: University of British Columbia Press, 2006).

academic, but importantly, does not take instructions from judges on what "spin" to put on the cases. The rationale behind the position is that the ELO's expertise should help make the journalists' job much easier, but also result in more informed and sophisticated analyses being presented to the public in the coverage of the decisions. The ELO conducts pre-session briefings to the media in order to highlight certain cases; briefings on judgements on appeal; media requests for interviews; and what are called "lock-ups".

In 2003, the Supreme Court of Canada became the first high court in the world to put into place a lock-up system. In order to recognize the imperative that journalists are under for almost instant communication of information, there is a one-hour blackout period where reporters are given a decision in advance of its announcement by the court, in order to give them a "lead time" to read and interpret the decision more fully. During these briefings the ELO presents the case, provides historical, social and legal context, highlights key findings and even points out central passages. The ELO's briefings are always "off the record" but offer interpretive resources and context for journalists who attend them. Inevitably, journalists have come to rely quite heavily upon the ELO, and some concede that his or her "take" on the case has an impact on the subsequent media coverage. However, overall, most journalists seem to feel that the ELO does a very good job at presenting the cases without a partisan framing. The overall consensus among the various parties is that reporting on the Supreme Court of Canada and its decisions has been improved as a result of these various initiatives and the Canadian Court now claims that it is the most open high court in the world.[9]

At the provincial level changes are also afoot. Manitoba is exploring the possibility of permitting photographers and television cameras into its courts, and the judges of that province have struck a committee to examine the issue. The New Brunswick Justice Minister suggested in 2009 that he was not eager to allow cameras into New Brunswick trial courtrooms, fearing the spectre of a move towards an "American-style justice system". However, cameras have been permitted at the New Brunswick Court of Appeal and in one case, the CBC was permitted to stream live footage to the Internet. British Columbia and Nova Scotia permit cameras in some courtrooms with permission and in Newfoundland, cameras are allowed in the courtroom until the judge enters. Most provinces have had isolated experiences where a judge has permitted some visual form of mediation in a proceeding and most of these have transpired without incident. In 1990, for example, the Manitoba Court of Queen's Bench provided for the taping, but not broadcasting, of all

---

[9]   *Ibid.*

criminal trials. Both CTV and CBC have been allowed to broadcast portions of hearings and trials, always with permission of the particular judge hearing the case. From 1995 to 1997, the Federal Court of Appeal also experimented with electronic access.

In 2005, the Ontario government created a Panel on Justice and the Media with the mandate to "define the challenges and appropriate roles of the media in a 21st century justice system". That body's 2006 report recommended sweeping changes to the ways in which Ontario handles the relationship between media and courts, and the Ontario government has acted quickly on a number of the recommendations. The recommendations were framed against five principles that speak more broadly to the issue of courts and the media and are guidelines likely to influence all courts. *Openness* to the public and media to court proceedings and records is to be promoted; procedures around *access* should be clear, consistent and timely; *education* between the two professions (legal and media) is valuable; the media and the justice system, while not partners, should be understood as *equal yet independent players*; and finally, the *privacy* rights of vulnerable people within the legal system must be respected. The report's diagnostic suggested that Ontario's courts lag behind many other jurisdictions in all aspects of media relations and access.

While the Panel was not prepared to open up the trial process to broadcast journalism, recognizing that as a still fraught issue, it did suggest that for all hearings where there are no witnesses, the benefits of openness from televising outweigh the concerns and therefore should be adopted. It recommended a procedure of lock-ups at the Court of Appeal level, similar to that in place at the Supreme Court of Canada. As a result of this policy review, Ontario began televising Court of Appeal cases in 2007 as part of a pilot project.

In most instances, the embrace of cameras has been in the context of appellate courts. They preside over appeals, not trials. The contents of appeals are typically legal arguments presented by lawyers to a panel of judges. There are no witnesses crying on the stand under brutal cross-examination; there are no impassioned addresses to the jury; there are no photographs of horrific crimes presented. In short, appeals typically do not make particularly compelling television viewing. However, some of the Canadian experiments over the years have involved trials and no documented harm has resulted. And once a jurisdiction has permitted an experiment with mediated access to the courts, it has effectively accepted the idea as legitimate in principle. The experiment then can be understood as a means by which empirical data on the effects of the changes will be gathered so that the actual mechanisms and procedures of mediated access can be refined.

Perhaps ironically, just as the Canadian legal system seems to be wrapping its head around the issue of cameras in the courtroom, as we saw in two of the examples with which this chapter began, other forms of technology are also making significant incursions into the space of law. As we have seen in every issue where expression and the law intersect, the role of interactive, networked technology cannot be ignored. And this is nowhere more true than in the consideration of which media technologies should be permitted to operate in the courtroom. The possibilities for the transmission of content from a courtroom to the public and for bringing non-legally sanctioned information into the courtroom posed by devices such as camera cellphones, Blackberries, iPhones and other handheld devices, social media such as Facebook, Twitter and YouTube and digital information portals such as Yahoo! and Google, make the debates over television cameras in courts look antiquated and naïve. We live in a world where personal media sit alongside mass media. For example, bloggers can, and do, sit in hearings and send live reports to the Web. Journalists and members of the public using the software Twitter, send micro-reports or "Tweets" out of the courtroom to media websites, listservs, personal websites or blogs, and through email to friends and acquaintances. Members of the public are wearing small wireless devices to stream continuous live video or audio onto the Web. These practices are happening despite the presence, in some instances, even of publication bans, let alone the courtroom restrictions on recording devices. Unlike television cameras, which are highly recognizable, it is much more difficult to police the use of small, unobtrusive mobile media technologies.

These practices are being felt most dramatically in the United States at present, where they are having a direct impact upon the legal system as we saw in the opening examples. Canada is not immune, however, from the rise of mobile digital technologies. A British Columbia court restricts the use of cellular phones to the point of confiscating them and physically searching everyone who does not have a pre-approved security pass. At the same time, not all courts are interpreting the technology as a threat. Some judges in the United States are beginning to permit online streaming of their proceedings and journalists' Tweets. Journalists claim that Twitter is best understood as another form of reporting the news that lends itself particularly well to legal reporting where a live camera feed is prohibited, as it provides immediate details from the courtroom as a dramatic trial unfolds. In 2007, bloggers who were covering the 2007 CIA leak trial of I. Lewis ("Scooter") Libby were given the same credentials as traditional journalists.

What we are seeing here is not just the infiltration of new media technologies into the courtroom, although that is certainly taking place. We are also seeing the entry into the courtroom of a different information sensibility. It is a sensibility that demands immediacy and intimacy in mediated content, that has less respect for the traditional boundaries of social institutions and is more actively engaged in their scrutiny, and one that has a more fluid notion of who its information providers are and should be. In other words, the expectation is that new information is going to be available simultaneously with the transpiring of the event, and that the content is less formal in its presentation. People are now consuming a wide array of informational content from a variety of sources, and the legitimacy of that information is not determined by the professional journalism credentials of its author. The boundaries between who is a producer and who is a consumer of information have changed and this has led, in some instances, to the empowerment of ordinary members of the public to become more active in scrutinizing social institutions — government agencies, Parliament, courts, school boards — and participating in the production of an information web around them. There is a change in orientation that results. In general, the mainstream media commentators have treated the courts with respect and a certain amount of deference. Amateur journalists and legal bloggers feel no such professional or cultural constraints, and nor do their readers expect or desire them.

This new sensibility also leads to members of the public who are less able to discern the quality of information that they are receiving (or are less concerned about that issue). These individuals are correspondingly rarely surprised or challenged in their news consumption because they deliberately seek out sources that support their own already-held views. In some senses, the debate mirrors the early arguments regarding television cameras in the courtrooms — while the technology has a greater capacity to inform the public and let the public assess the law for themselves, at the same time, there is a substantial risk that the nature of the medium itself and how we use it will lower the overall quality of the resulting discussion.

So, what does all of this mean for the ways in which the law expresses itself to the public? The final report of Ontario's Panel on Justice and the Media (2007) stated that "[t]echnology offers the justice-media relationship many opportunities."[10] In many ways, the new media sensibility held by members of the public, and also by journalists, has a democratic impetus. It certainly means that the issue of media in the courtroom is not subsumed by the issue of television cameras. It also likely signifies an increased trend towards more electronic transmission of legal information at all levels of courts, including even criminal trial courts. At the same time, resistance to these trends will not cease. For example, the

---

[10] See online: <http://www.attorneygeneral.jus.gov.on.ca/english/about/pubs/pjm>.

Recording Industry Association of America (RIAA), globally infamous for its legal pursuit of those file-sharing music, has launched an appeal of a 2009 decision to allow a webcast of a Boston hearing in a music downloading lawsuit. The RIAA is arguing that the webcast will violate Federal Court guidelines and threaten its ability to receive a fair trial. Journalists' organizations are defending the webcast in the public interest and as a free speech issue. It is one of the first of what will be many similar challenges in the United States and Canada as we begin to make sense of, and reach consensus on, the ways in which digital communications technology, information producers (professional and amateur) and the courts intersect.

III. LAW IN THE NEWS

In the fast-paced, visually dominated, affect-laden modern media environment, the complexities and technical nature of legal knowledge can pose a challenge to journalists, as we have seen. How do they turn something that might be considered "boring" or "technical" into something that will capture the public's attention and imagination, particularly when, as we have seen above, the ability to obtain visuals or video footage remains circumscribed in Canada? As well, complicated legal decisions do not lend themselves well to the "sound byte" style of television news reporting, in particular, where most stories are told in only two or three minutes or less. Television is also episodic rather than thematic, leading to a focus on events and individuals over larger themes and broader social issues. Notwithstanding these limitations, reporting on legal matters has increased in recent decades in Canada, particularly in relation to the reporting of crime. This is in part due to a continued public appetite for stories with conflict and drama, but also as a result of the demands for content of the 24-hour news cycle and the explosion of the televisual universe.

As with all news reporting, journalists use "frames" to tell the story of a particular legal dispute. Media scholar Todd Gitlin suggests that "[f]rames are principles of selection, emphasis and presentation composed of little tactic theories about what exists, what happens, and what matters."[11] These frames are particular ways of telling a story which highlight certain themes, certain actors, and certain events in a way that is recognizable to audience members. They assist us in organizing our

---

[11] Gitlin, Todd. *The Whole World is Watching: Mass Media in the Making and Unmaking of the New Left* (Berkeley, CA: University of California Press, 2003) at 6.

reality. For example, a frame of "David and Goliath" might be adopted in order to tell the story of an elderly woman pursued by the Coca-Cola company for trademark infringement when she posted details of her vintage Coke bottle collection on a website. The frame would highlight the woman's role as a vulnerable and weaker party who has done little, if anything, wrong and being oppressed by a much stronger international corporate conglomerate. The framing would invoke sympathy for the woman and anger at Coca-Cola Inc. It will shape who is interviewed as an expert and how the law is interpreted by consumers as just or not. Such frames permit news to be prepared and consumed more quickly through a shared meaningful framework that is already established; as a result, each event does not require its own specific narrative to be comprehensible. Often these frames are morally inflected, and are essentially tales of "good guys" and "bad guys".

In the most extensive study of legal journalism ever conducted in Canada, Florian Sauvageau *et al.* explored the pressures and challenges faced by both journalists and participants in the legal system, particularly judges, in relation to how legal decisions are reported in Canada. They focused their attention, in particular, on coverage of the Supreme Court of Canada in a variety of high-profile cases, and in the ways in which the Court was covered by the Canadian press from September 2000 to September 2001. It is important that we have Canadian studies of media coverage of the law, because our experience differs so much from that of our American neighbours, not only in terms of legal structure and the scope of the media industries, but also in tone and approach. Canada has not had a lot of what Mark Geragos has called "Supersized Trials" which place the ability of the accused to receive a fair trial at issue.[12] In general, journalists have been respectful and circumspect in their treatment of the personal lives and views of judges. Canada has also not identified a problem with what are known as "stealth jurors" — jurors who seek to be on a jury for ulterior motives usually involving conviction or attracting personal wealth and notoriety from media contracts. Finally, Canadians have shown little interest in saturation coverage of trials, the providing of up-to-the-minute and round-the-clock coverage of all aspects of a case with continual commentary and predictions from pundits.[13]

The findings in the Sauvageau study are instructive. In general, they confirm the findings of media scholars about how news is produced in general, according to professional norms, institutionalized practices and

---

[12] Geragos, Mark J. "The Thirteenth Juror: Media Coverage of Supersized Trials" (2007) 39 Loy. L.A.L. Rev. at 1167.

[13] The one exception to that might be the sentencing hearing of Karla Homolka and the trial of Paul Bernardo.

shared techniques. Those of their findings that inform our discussion of the ways in which the law is represented to the public are of two kinds: the structural attributes of the media-court relationship and patterns in the resulting content of news stories.

Legal reporting is a particularly unique kind of journalism where the reporter is often prevented from speaking to the major players in the process. Law is an expert domain of knowledge with a specialized language which the journalist is required to translate. Many cases do not offer compelling visual content and if they do, typically the journalist cannot film the proceedings or parties anyway. "The simple reality is that judgments that don't contain potent images are unlikely to become great TV stories even if they are crucial cases. Hence, the vast majority of cases will remain invisible, far below the waterline of public attention and knowledge."[14]

There are some structural factors which shape the way that legal matters are reported in the press. First, judges do not comment on decisions, before, during or after an appeal is heard. The legal decision, itself, is supposed to be the thoughts of the judges on the issues and so they are taken to have already said in writing everything they had to say about the case. This means, then, that journalists seek out the parties to the dispute, or interest groups on opposite sides of the issues in order to get quotations and responses for their articles and broadcasts. As well, journalism practice dictates a "pro versus con" or positive versus negative binary approach to issues. When decisions of the court are very close (5 to 4, for example), while the close decision is noted, it is rarely analyzed, as the focus turns to the pros and cons of the final decision (of the majority). Coverage is short — whether in newspapers or on television; complex issues must often be reduced to under 500 words or two minutes of speech. Finally, the nature of the coverage was significantly shaped by the fact that there are currently no reporters who have the Supreme Court as their "beat", namely who are assigned on a regular basis to cover the Court. Budget cuts in most major newspapers across the country have resulted in cutbacks to all areas of specialized reporting; only a few news outlets have journalists who specialize in legal matters at all. Often those charged with parliamentary matters double as legal reporters, as do those who cover crime issues.

These issues of structure impact significantly upon the ways in which legal decisions from the Supreme Court of Canada are reported and the patterns of representation contained in the coverage. Sauvageau and his colleagues found that a strong majority of the decisions released by the Supreme Court was covered in the press, and those not covered tended to

---

14   Sauvageau, *supra*.

be minor or contain technical decisions not likely to garner much attention. Certain high profile cases dominated the coverage and coverage almost inevitably clustered around the release of a decision. Cases involving high emotional content were most frequently picked up by television news; however, not surprisingly, given its limited visual appeal, generally there was far more coverage of Canada's highest court in newspapers than on television. Coverage focused almost exclusively on the official activities of the courts — such as decisions — and not on social issues associated with the legal system, the judges themselves, or the court as an institution. For example, there was widespread and significant coverage of the case of Robert Latimer — the Saskatchewan farmer who killed his severely disabled daughter — but virtually none of the symposium organized by the Court to mark its 125th anniversary. Yet these choices made by individual journalists and media organizations reflect the news values which privilege a story of conflict, tragedy and controversy over one of institutional history. Typically the cases which receive the most attention are those that play into established news values well, and are the most newsworthy. These are the cases that have key social debates at their foundation, have individually compelling characters in them, involve significant moral implications, are seen as key issues by the public, and those which garnered significant political attention. Yet, what is reported in the coverage is typically the decision itself, and its implications, rather than the reasoning behind the decision — a cause of frustration for some judges.

The researchers found interesting differences between coverage of the court in Quebec and in English Canada. Generally there is a greater amount of reporting on the court in English language news media, and French language coverage tends to take place when an issue before the court is of particular relevance for Quebec. However, when the court is covered in Quebec, it is done so just as favourably as in English Canada.

In general, the tone adopted towards the court was found to be neutral or balanced, with one exception. The *National Post*, particularly during the heyday of Conrad Black's proprietorship, engaged in regular and sometimes harsh criticism of what it considered the Court's judicial activism. In general however, the most common frame found by the researchers was that of politics. This meant that legal issues were translated into political terms and the issues became: assessments of the impacts of the decision on the government, calls on the government to act, conflicts between political parties and so on. As with any media framing, the selection of one frame precludes others, and so rarely were the decisions discussed in terms of ethical implications, situated in their historical context, discussed in legal terms, characterized as broad social justice issues and so on.

Coverage of the Supreme Court, then, in Canada is consistent with wider practices of reporting in general, and legal reporting in particular. Other than crime news, which often dominates screens and newspapers, particularly at the local level, the law tends to make the news just before, during and for a short period after a significant legal decision is released, provincially or nationally. What is a significant legal decision for the news media is not always the same as it is for lawyers, although there is often overlap. Coverage favours dramatic, conflict-based human stories with easily recognizable (and thus representable) protagonists and antagonists. The political effects of major Supreme Court of Canada decisions are those focused on by journalists in this era of judicial review.

Interestingly, what the study completed by Sauvageau and his colleagues, as well as other work on the representation of law in Canadian media, do not reveal is a series of ongoing and problematic distortions. Occasionally, in their haste, the media do "get it wrong", and there are certainly limits to the coverage as discussed above. However, overall, journalists and court officials seem to be working effectively to keep Canadians relatively well-informed about their legal system. This may be somewhat less true however of other mediated representations of the law as we explore in the next section.

IV. LAW IN POPULAR CULTURE

Representations of law have never been more popular with the public. From television shows like *Divorce Court, CSI* or *Boston Legal* to films such as *The Verdict, I am Sam* and the *Legally Blonde* films, our popular culture landscape is replete with narratives about law, lawyers, crimes, police and the legal system. This is true across a range of genres from reality television, to police procedurals, to ensemble dramas, to lawyer shows and across a range of media. Notorious trials are more popular than ever, making appearances not only in news reports, but in other media genres such as tabloids, docu-dramas and thinly veiled imitations of reality within fictional dramas. But as we know, the law is a complicated business and how can it be represented accurately in 60 minutes less advertising time for television or one hour and 45 minutes for film? The short answer is that it cannot. Representations of law within popular culture rarely seek to be accurate representations of the legal system and its actors; what they seek to do is tell a good story. They do not have the same public interest imperative to inform the public that the news media do. Films and television entertain us, but that does not mean, of course, that they do not simultaneously inform us, just not in the same way that the news media do.

While a growing number of scholars are turning their attention to the ways in which the legal system is represented in popular culture, the analyses are still overwhelmed by laments for a lack of accuracy. Concern is repeatedly expressed that trials in "real life" are not that short, never that dramatic and are much more tedious. In real life, lawyers work with notes, are rarely disrespectful to the bench and do not raise nearly so many objections. In real life, witnesses rarely break down on the stand, every criminal trial is not a jury trial, courtrooms are much smaller and lawyers never ask a question to which they do not already know the answer, and so on. These observations are correct; the ways in which popular culture texts represent the legal process is much higher on drama and excitement and much lower on tedium and routine than is the case in any actual legal system. The reason for the concerns expressed with the gap between fiction and reality is that popular culture narratives produce in viewers a distorted sense of how the law works and a false set of expectations of legal institutions and actors. This fear is heightened in the case of the Canadian instance, because most of our popular media content comes from the American cultural industries, and the Unites States' legal system is very different from our own. In Canada, we have a right to freedom of expression, not free speech; when we are informed of our rights upon arrest, it is not a "Miranda" warning; we cannot "plead the fifth" and so on. Thus, the content is doubly inaccurate in that it is not realistic and then again because it is dominated by American law.

This concern for accuracy has a number of effects. First, it assumes that audience members believe that everything that they see on television is true, and have a limited capacity to place a fictional text in an appropriate context. A related concern is expressed that these misled members of the public are then serving as jury members and bringing these fiction-induced misapprehensions back into the formal legal system. This would seem to have been the concern of the judge in the third example with which this chapter began. Second, the over-emphasis on accuracy assumes that the primary task of popular culture narrative is to inform and not entertain, arguably something that would be disputed by most audience members as well as by cultural producers. Third and related to this, it is ultimately a denial of the social value of the popular culture text, in that it is being compared to serious journalism or high culture and being found wanting. Fourth, it assumes that we can trace a more-or-less direct influence between the act of viewing a particular media text and its effect on the viewer's beliefs and behaviours. Theories have been developed within a behaviourist lens, assuming that human behaviour is easily influenced, usually negatively by external forces, including the media. Demonstrating this link scientifically, however, has eluded media scholars for most of the last century. While many of these theories are unsubstantiated and are roundly critiqued, at the same time, few of us would suggest that viewing horrifying, frightening, hilarious or poignant entertainment media leaves us completely unmoved and unaffected. Fifth and finally, the abiding concern with accuracy assumes that it is, in fact, the most interesting issue. Other research has suggested that popular culture representations of law do have impacts on us, and do have something interesting to say, but that the issues are much more complex than the mere accurate representation of the legal system to the public.

One of the most interesting recent examples of this trend towards a concern with direct media effects is what is popularly known as the "CSI Effect". The *CSI* franchise, including *CSI: Crime Scene Investigation*, *CSI: New York* and *CSI: Miami* is a trio of television series focusing on the work of crime scene investigators in three cities, Las Vegas, New York and Miami, respectively. They seemingly open a window into the black box, not merely of police work, but of the laboratory-based forensic investigation of crimes. Episodes are peppered with DNA swabs, bullet trajectory models, measurements of blood and tissue spatter, evaluations of carbon residue after the firing of a gun and the life cycles of insects that eat deteriorating human flesh. The heroes of the stories are the "geeks" — the forensic scientists who in the televisual world are fashionable, carry guns, and toil not only in the lab but in the mean streets, local swamps and nearby deserts. The original series debuted in 2000, with *CSI Miami* following in 2002 and *CSI New York* in 2004. They have been popular and are available daily in cable syndication.

Pertinent for our purposes, however, are the claims made about the effects of this show on the viewing public: the CSI Effect. There are three major impacts that some researchers have alleged.[15] The first is the Prosecutor's Effect, which is that the public has come to have very unreal expectations of the state and the prosecutor's office with respect to producing forensic evidence at trial. On CSI series, every trial not only contains, but in fact turns on, forensic evidence. In contrast, in real life, prosecutors' offices do not always have the time or budget to obtain forensic evidence, and it is not always available in the case at hand. The fear is that juries will begin to wrongly acquit criminals if there is no forensic evidence in the case. The second component of the CSI Effect is — the "Defendants' Effect" — the general perception that science is infallible. In opposition to the first claim, the fear here is that if the prosecution tenders forensic evidence, then jurors will be biased towards conviction, viewing the forensic evidence as unassailable, as

---

15 Podlas, Kimberlianne. "'The CSI Effect': Exposing the Media Myth" (2006) 16 Fordham I.P. Media (Ent. L.J.) at 429.

always true. The third effect is that the series provides knowledge to the viewer, making technical findings of evidence presentation more accessible to jurors. The result has been, claims this effect, that there is an increased public interest in the collection of evidence, in jury duty, and in careers within criminology and forensics. (This argument is not dissimilar from that made about increases in law school applications in the 1980s in light of popular television series such as *L.A. Law* and *Law and Order*.) The claims for this educational effect are extended past jurors and students to also encompass criminals who are now, apparently, more savvy in cleaning up the forensic traces of their crimes.

Empirical researchers trying to demonstrate or dispute the veracity of the CSI Effects are at odds, and remain caught in the conundrum that faces anyone attempting to establish a direct link between media content and behavioural shifts. Most of the research is anecdotal; worries are expressed by officials in the legal system about these possible effects — defence lawyers, judges and prosecutors, in particular. And so in sum, the CSI Effects are not likely as direct or as strong as claimed by proponents. However, there is likely no disputing that interest in forensic evidentiary practices has increased in the population at large. Because these shows fit into a larger cultural moment of the simultaneous fear of, and faith in, genetic technology, the texts might well be most effective in a general way in promoting science as a powerful mechanism in the search for truth.

Other scholars have taken up the challenge of mapping some of the more subtle and less direct impacts that law in popular culture might have on the public imagination. Scholar Elayne Rapping has argued that crime drama serves a ritualistic function for its viewers, allowing us to experience the threat of violence, but then be reassured by its containment at the conclusion of the dramatic narrative.[16] She suggests that while early televised crime dramas focused on legal crusaders working for the innocent, the current trend is a focus on crime control with players in the legal system protecting ordinary citizens from the deviant and the outsider. Ultimately, these narratives propagate an uncritical sense that order can and will be resolved through law, but also reveal to us that the threat to social order has shifted in our post 9-11 world. David Ray Papke suggests that what is most important about the popular culture trial is not its many inaccuracies, but rather the overall sense of the abstract concept of "the law" that it generates for viewers.[17] He argues that viewers are left with a sense of what it means to live under the rule of law. Still

---

[16] Rapping, Elayne. *Law and Justice As Seen on T.V.* (New York: New York University Press, 2003).

[17] Papke, David Ray. *Law, Cinema and Ideology in Hollywood Legal Films of the 1950s* (Los Angeles: University of California Press, 2001).

other scholars claim that in fact popular culture representations do not work to shore up values, but more productively to open them up to critique. Jeffrey E. argues that fictional narratives contrast the rule of law with the rule of man, suggesting that many nonlegal factors influence how the law operates.[18] He argues this is socially valuable. Popular culture therefore reveals that the law is not a stable, objective and neutral zone for the rendering of justice, but a much more human and complex set of interactions.

Others have argued that the moral lines of right and wrong are thrown into high relief when lawyers "go wrong" in the movies, or that the power within the legal system that can seem invisible if one is only reading judgements, is revealed in the drama of the narrative and the interaction of the characters on television. Some even go so far as to suggest that popular culture may offer a much-needed antidote to the flattened moral universe of law that is presented in many law schools in North America.

In a way, these other approaches to reading the way law is expressed in popular culture serve the valuable function of making visible the symbolic power of law, of thinking about law, not merely as a set of pre-defined institutions and practices whereby order is maintained and justice meted out, but rather as a site of cultural negotiation. Popular culture helps us to recognize legal culture as a culture, rather than as a set of self-evident truths. Popular culture legal narratives reveal broad tensions about gender in the legal profession and judiciary, allow us to examine the question of racial tensions in inner-cities, and reveal police, judges and lawyers as necessarily flawed human beings. They show us that we live in a risk society that requires us to take responsibility for our own social well-being. Popular representations can have a hegemonic effect, confirming the value of authority, stability and order in a society and linking the production of that with an ethically grounded legal system. At the same time, these narratives make an otherwise esoteric and largely remote institution such as the court system feel more available to us and thus more open to our engagement and critique. But what is evident is that in trying to understand how it is that we know the law, how the law is represented through various forms of media, it would be foolish to overlook that the single largest site of our consumption of information about the law and the legal system is popular culture.

---

[18]   Thomas, Jeffrey E. "Legal Culture and *The Practice*: A Postmodern Depiction of the Rule of Law" (2001), 48 *UCLA Law Review* 1495-1517.

V. CONCLUSION

How the law expresses itself in the public domain is both reflective and productive of how a society defines itself and its social values. The multiple ways in which public knowledge of law and the legal system are produced are important to understand, as they are at the heart of both the openness principle and the right of freedom of expression. Law and expression intersect around us every day in the news media — on television, in newspapers, and in Wikis, podcasts and blogs — and the shape of that news is determined, to a large extent, by the relationship the courts have with communications technologies. But on any given day when the Supreme Court of Canada or a Provincial Court of Appeal is not handing down a major and controversial decision, most of us are exposed to representations of the law through a variety of popular culture narratives. For better or for worse, these are an incredibly significant means through which the law is expressed to the citizen. And these mechanisms of public and popular communication are, for most members of the public, the primary means through which they experience and encounter the law. It is often through the cultural tools of mediated and popular legal narratives that we engage with the law, think critically about it, and form our expectations of it.

Yet, as became evident in the discussion of media technologies in the courtroom, the public sensibility towards news and information, and correspondingly towards traditional social institutions and actors, such as courts, judges and the legal system, is changing rapidly. Citizens expect their information immediately, forcing journalists to try to digest complex legal decisions in mere minutes or increasingly to send comments directly from the courtroom in real time. The rationales for why information cannot be transmitted freely from a courtroom, are less persuasive to a generation fully implicated in the use of mobile digital technologies than they are to the generation that comprises the senior judiciary. More and more people feel empowered to comment on their world and to share that communication with others, even if it has not been vetted by traditional mechanisms of knowledge-making or does not defer to those in positions of authority. Traditional knowledge-producers are having to adapt just as quickly as laypeople to the technological and cultural environment in which they find themselves, but in this, the court may be falling behind. It remains to be seen how Canadian courts will strike a balance between the openness principle, the freedom of expression of journalists and citizens, and the administration of justice. It is certain that there will be changes, the seeds of which have already been planted.

Chapter 6

Law's Expression, Looking Forward

I. LAW'S EXPRESSION

In April 2009 Swedish courts convicted the operators of a major bitTorrent file-sharing site operating out of Sweden of copyright infringement, making instant headlines around the world. Each individual founder of the site was sentenced to one year in jail and together they were fined 30 million Swedish kronor (approximately $4.3 million Canadian). The Pirate Bay site — well known to music file-sharers around the world — was allegedly responsible for approximately 50 per cent of the global bitTorrent traffic. Not surprisingly, the founders claim they will appeal the decision. Music industry officials hail this as a long-awaited victory, while others suggest that despite the decision (which might change on appeal), this does not mean that suing file-sharing members of the public is the most effective mechanism to deal with the challenges that digital technology have posed in the music domain. In fact, the decision comes after the Recording Industry Association of America (RIAA) recently announced that it was finally abandoning lawsuits against file-sharers as a strategy. And as we saw in Chapter 3, the Canadian Recording Industry Association (CRIA) had not met with much success in suing users either.

This example, while pertaining to the legal domain of copyright, highlights a number of broader themes that have arisen in this text across a wide variety of social and legal sites. Of course, it helps us to recognize the incredible impact that digital technology is having on the ways in which everyday people around the world are accessing, circulating and consuming their media. It shows us that formal laws attempt to control some of the ways in which we express ourselves, sometimes even to the point of invoking the criminal law or sanctions borrowed from criminal law. The example illustrates that those with substantial economic power sometimes have to take account of the practices of expression in which ordinary people engage and that the flow of influence is never unidirectional. The huge international media response to the case demonstrates an increasing awareness of communications law on the part of citizens and the fact that the law is frequently "news".

Importantly, the Pirate Bay case exemplifies the gap that exists between the control over forms and modes of expression sought by the law and the quotidian practices of citizens. That gap is sometimes temporal, in that the law is merely lagging behind the phenomenon that it is seeking to regulate. But sometimes that gap is conceptual, in that the law is operating upon a different logic than that of those it is attempting to govern. Both gaps are present here, and they confirm the convergence consciousness that has developed among media consumers in the past decade with its new attitude towards media industries, government regulation of communication, and our practices of producing, circulating and consuming information. Related to this, we can see that the ways in which legal issues impacting upon freedom of expression are never static. It is safe to say then that this example, as well as the many others we have taken up over the course of this book, effectively demonstrate that the stakes of human expression when it intersects with the law in a media society are very high.

Over the 1990s, many gurus predicted the demise of old media and the triumph of interactive new media. The Internet was going to replace our older ways of consuming information and there would be one black box in our home providing us with all of our communication services. It hasn't been quite so simple. The impact of new media has been huge, but it has not come at the expense of more traditional forms of media such as radio, television, film and even publishing. However, *how* these traditional communications media fit into our current mediascape, which is now shaped, not only by the dramatic rise of digital and mobile technologies, but also by what we have called cultural convergence, has changed radically. Regulators have had to adapt. We have many black boxes, many of them handheld, and we do not always consume our information in our homes. Just as the boundaries between types of media and content are blurring because of digitization, cultural convergence suggests that the boundaries between our strict identities as information consumers and other information producers is also blurring. We are engaged in the continual recirculation of content, in the production of social and personal media, as well as in more traditional practices of consumption, but on devices and at times of our own choosing.

Choice has become a hallmark value in the current mediascape and the more paternalistic forms of the regulation of communications technologies which favoured a set of assumptions anchored in the logic of cultural nationalism may seem dated to current consumers. Indeed, as we saw in Chapter 1, the regulatory logic in telecommunications and new media, in particular, has been moving towards increased global competitiveness. The Canadian Radio-television Telecommunications Commission (CRTC), as the national regulator of the communications infrastructure in Canada, is increasingly moving towards a more cooperative approach. However, the broadcasting regulatory structure is a bit of an anomaly, reflecting to a greater extent the ever-persistent cultural nationalist policy logic in an uneasy tension with deregulation and competition. Some might argue that the shift to deregulation is a move towards opening up the media terrain to greater freedom of expression, to the marketplace of ideas, whereas others will counter that the playing field in the marketplace of ideas have never been even and that Canadians sometimes need a boost.

The shift towards greater support for freedom of expression manifests in other areas of law that we have studied. A number of commentators suggested in the 1980s that the legal context in which journalists worked at the time was chilling. Laws such as contempt and defamation were vague and the perception was that courts favoured the accused's right to a fair trial, almost automatically, over the right of freedom of expression being exercised by journalists and media organizations. One can no longer make that claim. A series of decisions of the Supreme Court of Canada (as well as inferior courts across the country), a higher level of activism on the part of Canadian media organizations, technological developments and policy changes have combined to shift the balance towards much greater openness and much greater access by the media. Publication bans are increasingly rare and have to be justified more rigorously. Mandatory publication bans, provided for in statutes, are also under attack pursuant to section 2(b) of the *Charter*.[1] The place of journalists in society and the protection of the professional protocols through which they do their jobs are being granted more deference by Canadian courts than ever before. Greater protection of the confidentiality of the source-reporter relationship in recent years is a clear marker of this.

Yet, as with other areas of the law, we see the expansion of these issues beyond the original parties to the socio-legal transaction. Publication bans, confidentiality and defamation trials used to be battles between journalists (representing democracy and the public interest) and the courts (representing the justice system and the rights of the parties within it). With the participation in information production and circulation practices of non-professionals — amateur journalists we might call them — these new actors are implicated in publication bans and defamation disputes, in particular. Blogs, listservs, social networking media sites and so on are, among other things, opening up individual communicators who are not professional journalists to legal sanction.

Users of media are also "pushing the envelope" in the area of intellectual property law, and specifically copyrights and trademarks. While few of us would deny a creator the opportunity to profit from their labour and

---

[1] Part I of *The Constitution Act*, being Schedule B to the *Canada Act 1982* (U.K.), 1982, c. 11.

to ensure that their work is treated with respect, many of us would not expect to have to give up our right to criticize, make parodies, transport content from one of our media devices to another and so on, in order to do so. Many of us would need to be convinced that a creator should receive absolute and exclusive property rights in their creation if those rights negatively impacted our own freedom of expression to a significant extent. And yet intellectual property owners are seeking to do just that.

In the domain of copyright, there are significant international pressures on Canada to strengthen owners' rights through a variety of mechanisms, as the United States has done. For reasons that are ultimately unknowable, the Canadian government has not done so. As a result, it is repeatedly castigated by the American government and media industry lobby groups, described as a haven for pirates and criminals, a covenant-breaker, and a backward nation on intellectual property issues. Whether the Canadian government's legislative inaction is as a result of apathy or incompetence, or whether it is a more deliberate strategy of contemplation and compromise, is difficult to say. However, the result has been that Canada has not rushed ahead with hasty and ill-conceived amendments to its copyright regime. Instead, we have seen the coalescing of a network of interest groups which have become active in the consultation processes, we have seen a back-and-forth between draft legislation, industry players, users and critics which has resulted in change and compromise, and we have seen the awareness of the Canadian public on issues of copyright and their relevance to each of us escalate dramatically.

Along the way, the Canadian Supreme Court has been quietly but effectively confirming the basic principles upon which copyright in the digital age will be interpreted: including balance among users' and creators' interests; the support of a public interest in the copyright bargain; and understanding copyright as a means by which information and cultural content is encouraged, not discouraged, from flowing. These principles would seem to also be shaping the domain of trademark law in Canada, where again the high court has confirmed that it will not permit the domination of large corporate players at the expense of the consumer or the small business enterprise. Trademark law is first and foremost consumer law, and the trademark itself is not the product, even in our current brand society. The specific intersection of freedom of expression of ordinary citizens engaged in political speech and criticism and the limits that owners of trademarks can place on the use of their marks in a non-business context is winding its way towards Canadian courts, and will give the Supreme Court of Canada (if the case goes that far) an opportunity to fully articulate the parameters of the free expression-intellectual property relationship.

Thus, we have seen the Supreme Court be active in finding certain limits on freedom of expression unconstitutional, such as mandatory publication bans, and in opening up the terrain of mediated communication to greater freedom of expression by relaxing strictures on journalist-source confidentiality and defamation defences. In the area of intellectual property, we have seen the courts advocate very strongly for users and their rights to free expression. And in the area of the communications regulatory structures, we have seen the government, through its regulatory agency, the CRTC, take an increasingly "hands-off" approach to how media organizations and service providers operate the domain in which we communicate. As well, the government has not submitted to the file-sharing moral panic and passed rushed legislation. However, in the area of criminalized expression, none of these trends are visible.

On the contrary, we have seen greater, rather than less, government intervention into the issue. Canada adopted criminal legislation for hate speech, for example, breaking ranks with most other Western nations. While the legislative process in the domains of obscenity, child pornography and hate speech have been fraught, in the instances of both child pornography and hate speech, the ultimate legislation passed was done quickly and over significant concerns on the part of civil society groups and citizens. As well, the courts have been far less willing to find these provisions unconstitutional than they have been in the other areas of law we have explored. The Supreme Court, in particular, seems reticent to challenge the basic premises of the criminalization of these three forms of speech, and has rather opted to soften some of the more extreme elements of the legislative provisions with exceptions and qualifications that it has read into the *Criminal Code*.[2]

The Canadian government has historically been very reluctant to regulate newspapers, worried that it would be accused of being propagandist and of censoring the fourth estate, necessary to the proper functioning of democracy. It has been less concerned, seemingly, about the claims of censorship that have been levelled against it in the criminalization of certain marginal forms of speech. However, what this book has suggested is most interesting about the battles over obscenity, child pornography and hate speech is the ways in which those very disputes are constitutive of Canadian political identity. Through our ongoing negotiation of what is and is not acceptable communication within the polity, we make visible the fault lines and characteristics of the Canadian national character (in all its diversity). As well, certain forms

---

[2] R.S.C. 1985, c. C-46.

of criminalized expression are productive of other forms of community within the nation as well. Minority communities and their members both use certain forms of non-mainstream expression in the constitution of their identities, but also are defined, in part, in the clashes with the mainstream over those same forms of expression.

Finally, we might ask ourselves where and how the battles taking place over criminal speech help define communities — national and minority. We might ask how it is that awareness of copyright issues has soared in the Canadian population. We might ask how it is that the openness principle of courtrooms is made relevant to us when we have never stepped foot in a courthouse. We might ask how it is that we understand ourselves as legal subjects and develop a relationship with the law, even if we have not been arrested or sued pursuant to the law. The answers to all of these questions would no doubt include the realization that the legal knowledge of citizens is shaped, to a significant degree, by the ways in which the law is communicated to us. This communication takes place from professional journalists in the formal reporting of cases in the news, it takes place in the blogs and tweets of those who follow legal hearings and trials, and it takes place in the popular entertainment that we consume, a striking amount of which focuses on legal issues.

In other words, legal stories are all around us and thus if we want to better understand how it is that we know the law, we need to examine how law expresses itself. And this process is, as we saw, also not immune from the developments of new technologies. While historically, the debates about access to the courtroom had been focused on camera technology, this has quickly been overtaken by new media technologies and practices which are opening up the law to ever greater scrutiny. Some analysts and legal system participants think that this is a positive development and the more avenues through which the public can be exposed to the law, the better. Others are more cautious, worried that the values of the legal system differ from both those of journalism and the entertainment industry, and that those values may get lost in the rush to mediate. Regardless of one's position in the debate, the clear trend has been that courts have had to respond, not only to the technologies that threaten their control of the legal space of the courtroom, but to the public demand for more immediate and intimate forms of communication about legal matters. As we could also see in Chapter 2, the legal system cannot remain closed in our current media society and the effects of this opening up, voluntary or not, will be interesting to watch.

II. LOOKING FORWARD

Predictions as to the future outcomes of the appeal of the Pirate Bay case, of the CanWest trademark dispute with its social-activist critics, of the recent copyright consultations and the upcoming legislative amendments, the future of mandatory publication bans, the results of both the telecommunications and broadcasting policy reviews that are currently under way, the constitutionality of our hate speech provisions with a changed membership of Canada's high court, the CRTC's rethinking of new media regulation, or what the next "hot" development in digital technology or social networking will be, would be futile. As has hopefully become apparent over the course of this text, expression is a volatile activity that can never be fully controlled by law and regulation. It is unpredictable as, ultimately, are the social actors involved in the various free expression debates. As we noted at the outset, our forms of expression always leak out of the fences that we put around them. However, rather than making predictions which when accurate seem obvious in retrospect, and when wrong, look naïve or foolish, I will offer a series of seven principles that I am prepared to say will (and should) continue to shape the terrain of expression's encounter with the law. Hopefully they can guide us as students of communication, law and media as we move forward into the exciting developments that lie ahead.

First, expression has been, is, and will continue to be a fundamental human activity which is highly valued in democratic societies. In general, its place in our current environment, particularly conceived of as an individual right, is on the rise. An increasing number of the legal and social disputes through which we will define the shape of our society and our roles within it, will involve the effects of various individuals, groups and institutions encountering limits placed on their free expression.

Second, it is important to remember that issues of freedom of expression are not just the concerns of journalists, media owners, music producers, pornographers and painters. In part because freedom of expression includes not only the act of communicating, but that of receiving information, of listening, of being informed about public affairs, it is relevant to us, even when it is others doing the communicating. However, increasingly, many more of us are finding ourselves communicating, not just to colleagues, friends and families along personal and work channels, but to much broader publics through a variety of new media technologies and applications. We are expressing ourselves in whole new ways that are intersecting with the legal restraints on communication in an interesting manner. No longer are we merely information consumers; we are producers and distributors as well. Freedom of expression matters to all of us.

Third, parallel to the above democratization of the practice of expression in the public domain, we are also witnessing an ongoing democratization of legal knowledge as well. Information about law is available to us 24 hours a day and we are demanding even more. We are increasingly aware of our rights to communicate, and are correspondingly distrustful of those that would limit that expression. This emergent communications consciousness will only continue to grow and develop and will shape the nature of our legal disputes in ways more potent and powerful than will technological developments alone.

Fourth, these processes of democratization noted above are resulting in our recognition of the porous nature of most of the traditional boundaries through which we have structured the communications technological and legal-regulatory infrastructures. It is not so easy to distinguish any longer between content and carriage, between who is a broadcaster and who is a telecommunications service provider. It is not so easy to distinguish between who is a professional journalist and who is a blogger. It is not so easy to distinguish between who is a producer of media and who is a consumer. Various hybrid identities, practices and technologies are emerging that resist the traditional frames in which we place them, forcing those frames to change. Change has become the new norm.

Fifth, in our increased scrutiny of the limits placed on freedom of expression in our society must come a related awareness that censorship is alive and well in Canadian society, that this might not always be a completely negative thing, and that the threat of censorship is not only from, or perhaps even most powerfully from, the state. Censorship is one of the means through which we address the incredible power of expression to do not only good, but harm. Legal debates around it are constitutive of forms of identity and not merely constraining of them. However, censorship happens not only through express prohibitions from the state on what can and cannot be communicated, but also in funding programs to support industries, in the overzealous protection of intellectual property rights in industry, in the very digital code that comprises the social networking sites in which we so eagerly participate, and in the access we have through economic resources and contracts to the means of expression.

Sixth, it should be apparent upon completion of this text that Canada has its own unique approach to issues of freedom of expression and its legal constraint. Repeatedly, Canadian governments and courts have taken independent approaches to freedom of expression issues that affect not only the local and national, but global arenas. For the most part, Canada has not been bullied by its larger trading partners and their dominance of the international mediascape, and this is true historically as well as currently. Whatever choices Canadians, their courts, and their governments make in the future, they will continue to be shaped by a distinct, if undefinable, Canadian sensibility about how we do and should communicate.

Seventh and finally, when one is interested in issues of freedom of expression and its encounter with the law, one should not look only to legislation and case law. Freedom of expression and its disputes are all around us. They appear in courtrooms with striking regularity, but they are also on the CBC and CTV news at night, they are on our Facebook pages, they are in the emails we send at work, they are in the music we consume, they are in the cheap knock-off that we buy in New York, they are in the back corner of our magazine store, they are on *CSI: New York*. As scholars of communications and law it behooves us to look in all of these places if we truly want to understand law's expression.

Index